# KANCHI DOCTOR

# Kanchi Doctor

The story of
**Ruth Watson of Nepal**

by
**David B. G. Hawker**

**SCRIPTURE UNION**
130 City Road, London EC1V 2NJ

© David Hawker

First published 1984

ISBN 0 86201 217 1

Typesetting by Nuprint Services Ltd, Harpenden, Herts.
Printed and bound by Cox & Wyman Ltd, Reading.

# CONTENTS

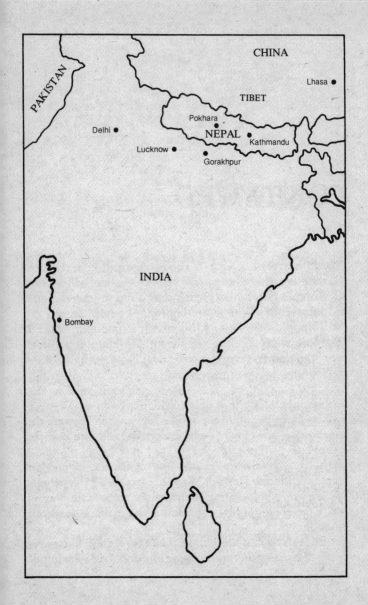

# FOREWORD

When I read the last pages of this manuscript, I put them on the table beside me and sat absolutely silent and still for two or three minutes. Tears were trickling down my cheeks, and I did not want to get up and return to my everyday world.

Through these pages I had visited a country to which I have longed to go since childhood. My journey to Nepal through the pages of this book did not disappoint me. It was a country as fascinating, oriental, mysterious, beautiful, ugly and haunting as I had always imagined it to be. The people and their culture were as different from my Western ways as I had thought they might be – and yet through the pages of this book I felt I could understand and even begin to love them.

In this book, through the eyes of the author and his incredible heroine Dr Ruth Watson, I travelled to Nepal over twenty-five years ago and watched the miraculous way in which God brought his church into being in that very special kingdom.

But this book is much more than a book about a country, or the fascinating and encouraging account of the founding of

God's church, it is the story of an incredible woman – Ruth Watson.

And, never having met Ruth before, through this book I felt I began to know her. But it isn't as simple as that. I worked for sixteen years as a missionary myself in South East Asia, and in those years I met women missionary doctors from many different countries. And in the story of Ruth Watson's life, I could also see the story of some of the other women doctors of her generation who pioneered missionary work of a calibre that would astound today's average short-term worker overseas.

Ruth Watson exhibited a commitment, a strength of character, a discipline and a devotion to Christ that will challenge and encourage young Christians today. And this biography about her is the more encouraging because it reveals her humanity – in common with other great people, she exhibits not only an extraordinary strength of character but the weaknesses that go hand in hand with particular strengths.

It was hard for this woman as a young doctor to pioneer work in Nepal, to establish a medical programme, and then as she grew older to face changes in thinking about what type of medicine was appropriate for Third World situations. She was a good doctor – and this was recognised by the Royal College of Surgeons who elected her as a Fellow (without examination) just before her death at the age of fifty.

To have read about Ruth Watson, for me, was to meet again some of those great women medical missionaries I have been privileged to know in the past. When I read the moving account of Ruth's death due to a brain cancer, I remembered the deaths of those particular missionary doctors who have been significant in my life.

For within this book there is more than the important biography of Ruth Watson – hidden within this book is a history of medical missions, how they were started, how they developed, tensions they faced, changes they faced, their joys, encouragements, griefs, and the people who gave their lives to serve God through their work. This book reminds me of an era in medical missionary work, in which I was privileged to serve for sixteen years, but which is now rapidly passing and (rightly) being replaced by preventive medicine and care at grass roots level. Nevertheless, the era of the world famous medical missionary hospitals is an important era in the history of missionary work. This book about Ruth Watson, I believe, accurately portrays that part of our history.

Anne Townsend
April 1984

# 1
# ARRIVING

Dirt. Flies. The overwhelming smell of garlic and spices.

These were Ruth Watson's first impressions as the SS Chusan berthed at Bombay.

The dock in the great city buzzed with life – shouting, struggling, even fighting for the right to carry baggage to the arrivals and customs shed. Hands, heads, noise everywhere. Scantily-clad labourers seeking the few rupees which might, for a day at least, separate satisfaction from hunger, life from death.

The journey had been superb. Two marvellous weeks. After the exhaustion of packing and last-minute shopping, and the final, tearful goodbyes and waves as the boat train left London, those days on board ship had been just what Ruth needed.

Time to recover, to enjoy the sun of the Mediterranean, to revel in the fascination of Egypt and its pyramids. Through the Suez Canal, along the Red Sea, and finally a long crossing over the Indian Ocean: time to prepare for the new life to which she had been called, time to study and pray with other missionaries sharing the journey.

And now India.

She watched, horrified, as luggage was unloaded from the hold in nets suspended from great cranes. Bicycles, sewing machines, boxes marked 'Glass, with care', were all jumbled in the net with heavy trunks and cases, and then unceremoniously dumped on the quayside. Watching the huge bundles crash to the ground, she wondered about the fate of her box of surgical instruments, china, and gifts for future colleagues.

Passport control was nothing if not thorough, beaten only for slowness by the customs officials. Everything must be opened, slowly explored, sometimes withdrawn and looked at in amazement.

'What is this, please? For why is it brought? How many do you have? Where is your husband?'.

Then the repacking – and all the time the scorching heat, eased little by the fans in the customs shed, brought its own problems.

'I'm thirsty, but the water isn't safe to drink. Look at all those flies. I'd better have tea. They say that is safe . . . I wonder.'

There was little time to acclimatise, or recover her land legs. Soon she was off again, heading north for the land-locked Himalayan country of Nepal, a train journey of 1,500 miles.

The monsoon was past, but the heat in the plains was still intense in the afternoons. Ruth travelled third class that first day of October. This was generally regarded as safest for women, and most trains had 'Women Only' compartments, which provided some shelter from the crowds who packed the train.

For Ruth, just twenty-six, and whose previous overseas travels had been limited to Western Europe, the journey was a dizzy kaleidoscope of stations packed with travellers, some standing, others squatting, sleeping or even dying on the platform which was their only home. Vendors selling all manner of fly-infested sweet meats, curried snacks, chapatis; the constant cry of 'Char, Char'; the tea served hot and sweet in disposable rough clay cups. A cacophony of sound coming from every direction. People getting on and off, simultaneously, through doors sometimes, through windows often. Clinging to the roofs, running boards, buffers. Everywhere packed solid with hot human flesh, and not a few animals. Such numbers, such need. Ruth's medical training had not included such extremes and volume of need. She knew it would be something like this, but the volume....

The pioneer spirit stirred within her; a determination and a love which resolved again to do all that she could, for as long as she could, for as many as she could. The God who had called her would enable her.

As she journeyed on, through the day and restless night, changing trains, hiring coolies to carry her luggage across the line between the platforms, looking for food, looking for toilets, there was something in Ruth which revelled in this. The sense that she was in the middle of God's plans enabled her to exult as she travelled towards Nepal. As yet she did not know that in the years to come that awareness of God's plans was to equip her to endure much more subtle and damaging assaults.

At Lucknow, in the elegant Victorian railway station, Ruth was met by Jean Raddon. She too was still learning her way round India, having arrived just a few months earlier. For twenty years they were to be close colleagues, with a growing respect for one another, despite occasional disagreements. But now, after two days on a hot crowded train, a friendly face came as a great relief to Ruth.

One missed connection, and one night in a waiting room found them at Gorakhpur boarding the even more crowded, dirty branch-line train for the final sixty-mile, four-hour journey to the border town of Nautanwa. Among their fellow travellers were many Nepalis, returning to their homeland after working in India.

Fifteen years earlier, on New Year's Day 1936, as a young missionary newly arrived in India, Lily O'Hanlon (also called Pat) had seen the distant mountains of Nepal whilst travelling in northern India. In that moment God spoke to her; one day she would enter that forbidden land, shut tight to all foreigners.

For fifteen long, hot, dusty years, joined by colleague Hilda Steele, she had waited in Nautanwa – a dirty, noisy and often immoral border town. Waited for the government of Nepal to change its policy and let foreigners in. Whilst they waited, they ran a small clinic to help Nepalis, mostly Gurkha pensioners who came to Nautanwa to collect their pensions. Slowly and patiently they made contacts, built relationships and collected a team to enter Nepal. With them was a small group of Christian Nepalis, exiled from their homeland because they had turned from Hinduism to Christianity. Thus the Nepal Evangelistic Band was formed – temporarily based in Nautanwa waiting for the door to open. And as they waited they ministered to the many Nepalis who poured through.

It was to join this small group of people that Ruth had left her home in the Midlands of England and the security of the medical profession.

As her train steamed into Nautanwa and Ruth joined the hordes of disembarking passengers on the platform, she knew nothing of what lay ahead. She knew only that after three days of continuous travelling she had arrived, baggage and all.

There, waiting to greet her and lead her away to much needed rest and refreshment, were Pat, Hilda and their Nepali colleagues.

A colleague recorded the event in her diary:

> The team is now complete. It was like a jigsaw puzzle trying to get ourselves and all our belongings in. It was Pat's birthday celebration and we drank tea from the beautiful cups Ruth had brought and ate her cake too. At 4.30 we had a communion service and then went for a walk across the fields. That night we had a special birthday supper with gifts for everyone, from England, Kalimpong and Patna. There were two pretty table-cloths and several practical little things – soap, tape, elastic and a nailbrush. And a bag of nuts! Two food parcels had arrived from Denmark. It was good to have something nice for the welcoming meal – we wanted to break Ruth in gently on the Hindustani food.

But her new colleagues could not shield Ruth completely from the traumas of beginning a new life in the East. It was not so much the crowds and flies and smells which affected Ruth. It was strange, small matters; like how to clean her teeth in the dark.

> I was petrified the first night I stayed in the bungalow, sleeping on a high verandah outside. The bathroom was down dark, difficult stairs, just a commode pot and a bucket of water. I didn't dare venture alone through the darkness. Somehow we couldn't express our fears in those days. I thought, 'But I'm a missionary now, and I shouldn't be afraid,' but I was. And I haven't cleaned my teeth at night for twenty-five years!

# 2
# NEPAL

Before February 1951 Nepal deliberately and rigorously isolated herself from the rest of the world. She had seen the expansionist, colonial activities of Britain in India, and was determined they should not happen in Nepal. Nepal lived quietly, a feudal backwater, largely unaffected by developments in the wider world. The rich grew richer and the poor lost hope. Politically she was free, but it was an empty freedom for the ordinary people.

Isolation could not continue for ever. When, in 1948, the British withdrew, having divided the sub-continent into the two parts of Pakistan and India, two thousand miles apart, political upheaval followed. The rulers of Nepal were not immune to the shocks. The time was ripe for change.

For more than a hundred years Nepal had been governed not by her king, but by a single family, the Ranas. Having gained power, they had relegated the king to the status of a figurehead, a virtual prisoner in his own palace. Jung Bahadur, the first of this line of hereditary prime ministers, was ambitious, selfish and ruthless, yet a man of much foresight and diplomacy. He visited Queen Victoria in London (no small journey in the 1850s), and this visit led to the founding of the Gurkha Brigade in the British Army. In 1857 he sent eight thousand men to fight for the British in the Indian Mutiny. He died an absolute dictator, and an extremely wealthy man.

This pattern continued and pressure for change built up inside and outside Nepal. In November 1950, King Tribhuvan, apparently setting out for a picnic with his family, went to the Indian Embassy, and asked for help in setting Nepal free from the tyranny of the Ranas.

The fuse had been lit. The king was flown to Delhi and civil war broke out on the borders. The Ranas stood down, and Tribhuvan returned to a tumultuous welcome on February 16th 1951.

With the country now open, the British appointed their first ambassador. The appointment proved to be enormously significant for the work of God in Nepal.

Early in 1951 Pat O'Hanlon and Hilda Steele were on furlough in Britain. They were invited to tea with Pat's former school teacher and she introduced them to her brother.

'I'd like you to come and meet my brother. He is going to Nepal as the new ambassador.'

So a vital link was forged. Sir Christopher Summerhayes and his wife became friends of the mission group. He invited Pat and Hilda to Kathmandu, and arranged meetings with the new Minister of Health, who was enthusiastic about their plan for a hospital. He gave permission and a three-day visa for a visit to Pokhara, and even arranged for them to travel aboard the king's Dakota aircraft, a journey of thirty-five minutes which would have taken nine days on foot! From there they trekked back to Nautanwa, and immediately applied to the Nepali Government for permission to work in Pokhara.

When Ruth arrived in Nautanwa a year later, final

permission had still not been received. The team gathered one cool October evening on the flat roof of the mission house – six missionaries and nineteen Nepalis – besieged by mosquitoes. The magnificent Himalayas glowed red in the setting sun sixty miles to the north. In their unhurried communion with God that night a quiet certainty came that the time was near. Unknown to them, the permission had already been dispatched from Kathmandu, and money sufficient for the initial days had been sent from the mission headquarters in Edinburgh.

Missionaries had entered Nepal before. Nearly two hundred years earlier a group of Roman Catholic Capuchin monks on the way to Tibet passed through Nepal. Their journey was long, arduous and dangerous. A number stopped in Kathmandu where they preached, socialised, helped and taught. Some brought medicines, others acted as mediators in local wars. They treated royalty and commoners alike. They were, as were the later missionaries, treated with a mixture of friendliness and generosity. In time eighty adults believed and were baptised.

The situation was short-lived. In 1723 Prithwi Narayan Shah was born. At the age of six he is said to have climbed a two-thousand foot ridge to the temple of Gorkhanath where, according to tradition, an old man, a manifestation of the Hindu god, prophesied his coming greatness. He grew up an ambitious man with iron will and nerves of steel, a natural leader and a fine organiser. He united the warring Nepali tribes, conquered all opposition and defeated the British, effectively ending the colonial threat.

Prithwi Narayan Shah was suspicious of the foreigners, accusing them of complicity in calling in the British army. He expelled the missionaries and the Nepali Christians. The valley was closed to foreigners. In the intervening centuries nothing happened. Nepal stood still and when the next missionaries entered all traces of the Capuchins, their writings, their crosses and their churches had totally vanished.

# 3
# ENTERING

November 10th 1952 was *the* day. Frustrating weeks after being told unofficially that permission to start medical work in Pokhara had been granted, the official letter eventually arrived. After just three weeks to get used to the new culture, Ruth Watson was on the move again.

As soon as the letter arrived, contact was made with the British Army Recruiting Centre just over the border in Nepal, at Paklihawa. Help was rapidly forthcoming, and on November 9th a three-ton lorry, with its driver, an army captain, and his second in command, arrived in Nautanwa, complete with a cooked chicken to make their final meal a good one.

The house was buzzing with activity. From the direction of the roof sounds of much laughter could be heard. Two people were busy packing last-minute things into their suitcases, while another two were struggling to fasten a fat and bulky-looking bedding roll.

Very little personal luggage was allowed initially, but it was obvious from the contours of the 'roll' that it contained other things besides bedding. Where else could they put those badminton rackets, the odd pyrex dish and shoes that might be needed on the journey? Packing complete at last, Joan Short sat wondering if she had done the right thing in choosing to wear her crepe sandals and pack her 'nails'. Ruth, however, had no difficulty at all in deciding what shoes to wear. Early in the morning she was already clonking around in heavy, professional-looking boots.

Meanwhile, down in the courtyard, Pastor David Mukhia, who was to remain in Nautanwa as their agent, was organising the five Nepalis who were to accompany them to Pokhara. The oldest of these, Priscilla, was stuffing all her possessions into a large, untidy-looking sack. There was a large frying-pan handle sticking out of the mouth of the sack. It was an unenviable burden for some unfortunate porter.

By 9.00 am the truck was loaded, and after much lurching and groaning it was off, swallowed up in great clouds of dust from the road. They took one and a half hours to cover six miles to the border along rutted roads and over the worst bridges Ruth had ever seen.

At Bhairawa they had a long wait at the Nepali customs shack, until after an hour and a half, the various items of luggage were individually sealed with minute red seals and an official pass issued. They were away, heading north inside Nepal.

For the first ten miles the land continued perfectly flat, entering the Nepali jungle of trees and undergrowth. To the north the foothills grew higher and closer, and the mighty Himalayas were lost to view behind them. By lunch-time they arrived, all eleven of them, in Butwal. Here the road ended. From here it was on foot, and porters had to be hired.

Pat and Hilda were having great difficulty hiring porters, not because there were none willing, but because they were asking a greatly inflated price. The first night was spent there, sleeping in the open, using the luggage as a windbreak and the wind to keep off the mosquitoes.

Ruth's diary records:

The first thing we did was to find some food and drink at an ex-patient's house. We had to eat with an audience of about thirty, plus several inquisitive goats, two of them just born. We are getting used to doing things in public.

Next morning they were up at five o'clock, had tea and biscuits and resumed the haggling. Eventually, to show they meant business, the whole party headed off north, leaving Pat and Hilda to finalise arrangements. Finally, nineteen porters were hired and soon the journey began in earnest. This was Ruth's first day of walking in Nepal, and she loved the beauty of the mountain path and the villages.

That evening we slept in a large house in Rhanibas. In that one room were the six of us, our five Nepali colleagues, eighteen porters, the owner, and a girl dying of TB. During the night one of the coolies began to sing and Pat had an attack of asthma and needed an injection. But we slept fairly well!

Then another early rising, followed immediately by a full meal of rice and lentils. The porters insisted on eating early, but the missionaries found it very hard to take in enough food to last twelve hours and still to walk. Nonetheless it was a beautiful day's walk.

We walked all day, over the first high ridge. What scenery! It is beyond all description. As we come to the top of each ridge we have a fresh vision of the snows getting nearer and nearer. Sunrise and sunset especially light up the hills and mountains in exquisite colours.

The pace was slow. Many of the women were very unused to this hill walking and the party was large, the porters carrying loads of up to one hundred pounds in baskets suspended from their foreheads. But the slow pace gave Ruth a chance to take in some of the geography of the land to which she had come.

The Himalayas are the youngest of the world's mountain ranges. Stretching for 1,500 miles, the range is often 10 miles wide and has 200 peaks higher than 23,000 feet. They are still growing by up to six inches a year in height, though much of that growth is lost by erosion.

The great land mass of the Indian subcontinent still moves northwards, its plates pressing against the static mass of central Asia. These movements result in frequent earth tremors and occasional major earthquakes, though because of the remoteness of the area, few are of serious consequence. In 1934, however, a major quake hit Kathmandu, destroying many buildings and killing thousands of people. Pokhara was also badly affected.

From the top of the ridges, Ruth could see hundreds of miles of Himalayan peaks to the north and, turning round, gazed southwards over the seemingly endless plains of India, where the sacred Ganges river, and its equally sacred tributaries, ran one thousand miles to the sea.

The trek took them through the valley below Tansen and they had to spend that night in a village miles from a water supply, in one small low-roofed room in which they cooked and slept. There was no chimney for the smoke. 'We all looked as if we had been weeping for weeks!'

Sleep was poor.

They were up at daybreak, had breakfast of bread, butter and marmalade with tea and left for the valley far below. There they stopped, bathed in the delightful cold water, ate rice and went on to Ramdighat.

Here, the Kali Gandaki river flows fast, cutting a deep gorge in its tortuous path to the Indian Plains. The river originates not in the Himalayas but in the true watershed for the region, the high Tibetan plateau, and to make the plains of India it must cut through the Himalayas, producing the most colossal gorge on earth as it hurtles down between the peaks of Dhaulagiri to its west and Annapurna to its east. They crossed the Kali Gandaki on a swaying suspension bridge high above the huge green river.

Ruth's diary is made up of the small but vivid impressions of the trek: the funeral pyres on the shores below, the abundance of November fruit — oranges, lemons, bananas and pineapples.

After Ramdighat the inevitable long, hot climb up again out of the valley towards the next ridge:

> On the way up this hill we passed a leper asylum. Oh, how terrible! We saw about forty lepers, men, women and children in all stages of the disease. They live in rows of mud houses and are given no medicine whatever and a food ration only now and again. Some soldiers are there to keep them from running away. How we longed to be able to help them.

These unfortunate people had, in fact, been transferred to this colony at Malunga from Pokhara when the people there had created such a fuss that the local governor had them moved. The Pokhara site lay barren until the Nepal Evangelistic Band took it over and gave new hope for leprosy sufferers.

Another day's walking through an area very short of wood and water brought them into a long valley where they stayed, resting over the Sunday.

> The valley had a swiftly flowing river running through it, with clear, deep pools, ideal for swimming. Alas, we could not swim because we were always surrounded by a great crowd of people. The valley is very fertile, and peppered with villages stretching up the hillsides. Most of the villages comprised about two dozen houses, their mud walls coloured a bright red, and with thatched roofs. Everywhere the red flashes of the poinsettias added more colour, and butterflies,

dragonflies and birds of every hue darted about as we walked along the track. A kingfisher flashed by, diving into the river looking for fish. In the morning, the valley was covered in a dense mist — very useful cover for our ablutions! It made a change from washing in the dark, trying to remember where one had put the soap and towel.

November 17th found the group climbing out of the valley and several thousand feet up to the last ridge. That night they slept right on top of the ridge on the verandah of a house. The cold night winds blew off the snows but Ruth snuggled down into her sleeping bag, thankful she had bought a good one. The trek was nearly over. Next morning they would make the final descent, into Pokhara, the place of promise and calling. Exhausted after eight days of walking and inadequate food, the group slept, thankful to their God for his protection and goodness.

These early pioneers, like the Capuchins before them, were not special people. They were flesh and blood, with normal human limitations. They did have special qualities, however, which marked them out from their fellow men and women: qualities of obedience to the God who called them, and determination, even stubbornness, to fulfil the call.

What were the factors and experiences in Ruth Watson's background which resulted in her, that November night, sleeping on a windy ridge above a remote, undeveloped Himalayan valley, eight thousand miles from home?

# 4
# ROOTS

Ruth was born in Coventry, in the industrial heartlands of England. Her father was a first-class engineer in the motor industry who had worked on the development of magnetos, and later fuel injection systems. During the war he worked secretly with Sir Frank Whittle on the development of the jet engine. His abilities were highly regarded, and even after his retirement from his post as Technical Director at Lucas he continued to give papers on engineering subjects.

He was a man of great drive and energy – an active man who rarely relaxed. Such were his powers of concentration and application that the children would often say 'Goodnight' to their father as he worked in his study, and go to bed, only to find him still at work in the morning.

His interests went beyond his engineering. He enjoyed hill walking and rock climbing and took excellent photographs. Above all he found gardening an interest which continued into old age.

Philosophically he had been greatly influenced by the Darwinian thinking of his parents. Believing in the ability of man to develop, evolve, and improve himself and his society, his system had little place for any concept of God. Like many others he was loath to become an atheist and formed a nominal attachment to the Unitarian Church.

Ruth's mother was a secretary before her marriage, a warm and affectionate woman. She and Dr Watson had four children. John, the eldest, followed in his father's footsteps. Colin, after wartime service in the Navy, became a farmer. Ruth, born on 16th September 1926, was the third, her sister Jill being born four years later.

Family life was fairly normal. Dr Watson spent little time with the children. He brought home the money in the desperate years of dark depression and his wife provided stability for the growing family. He did discuss scientific matters with John and later with Ruth but beyond that there was little communication. Both boys went to boarding school and Ruth journeyed ten miles by bus to Warwick. Though she earned a scholarship her father did not take it up, feeling he could afford to pay.

The children were taught that time was to be used. Like her father, Ruth felt the constant need to be doing something. In later years, Ruth was always to be found during any meeting with a bag of knitting. If she stopped knitting, you knew something serious was happening! She found it hard to sit back and relax. In the heat of Nepal, after a busy day, when others were slumping on their beds to recover, Ruth would be off visiting, or doing something 'necessary'. Without her realising it, this put pressure on her average colleagues who lacked her indefatigable energy.

The 1930s were dark years. Economic depression caused mass unemployment, and state aid was very limited. Medically too they were dark years. There were no antibiotics, or treatment for tuberculosis, the mass killer. For those with eyes to see, war clouds loomed darker year by year.

The Watson family was well protected from these bad times. Dr Watson had a steady job and the motor business was expanding. They were by no means well off, but with careful management they were able to save up enough to allow the family a holiday each year. Her father was a keen climber, and when she was old enough, Ruth used to accompany him on some of his expeditions. North Wales was not far, and, if care was taken to avoid the scree, there was excellent climbing. Ruth learned to use ropes and all the other paraphernalia which makes for exciting but safe climbing.

Then, when she was ten, Ruth had a mild attack of rheumatic fever. Rare today, it was then common. There was no penicillin to treat it, and bed and rest was the only cure. Ruth recovered well.

Partly because of her illness, Father took them ski-ing in Switzerland and Austria. Four winters were spent in the fine, clear air of the Alps, which proved a tonic for all, especially Colin and Ruth who were regarded as sickly. The outbreak of the Second World War ended these trips.

These were the outstanding memories of Ruth's childhood. Foreign travel added a whole new dimension to the experience of a growing youngster. Mountains and Ruth went together. Seeds were sown which bore fruit later on the slopes of the mighty Himalayas in a far distant and, at that time, unheard-of land.

Ruth was thirteen when war broke out. Coventry and other parts of the industrial Midlands were sure targets for enemy bombs, and so the family was evacuated. The boys were already away at school. Jill was sent to boarding school in mid-Wales, where she learnt very little. Ruth was barely affected. She was at King's High School for Girls in Warwick, so she went to stay with the family of one of her school friends. This parting with the added fears prompted by war may have helped to make the parting years later a little less traumatic.

The friend's father was vicar of a parish in Warwick. Ruth and Jill had gone to Sunday School for a time whilst in Coventry – the done thing in those days – and whilst staying in the vicarage, Ruth was confirmed into the Church of England. Her teenage excursion into organised religion had little lasting impact on her, however, and by the time she reached the sixth form her views were radical and left wing. She wanted something better than the bombs and blackouts, sirens and mass destruction all around her.

These views, however, were to change. In her final year two major decisions were made which were to alter the whole course of her life. The first was to study medicine. She applied to Birmingham University Medical School and was accepted.

The second was even more significant.

The summer following the end of her school days Ruth joined a school friend on a camping holiday. The camp was run by the Girls' Crusader Union, and while Ruth had no interest in Christianity, she did like outdoor life. She went, determined to enjoy herself, and equally determined to take no notice of the Christian talks.

Unfortunately she became ill during camp, probably with a recurrence of the rheumatic fever she had suffered earlier. She was stopped in her tracks and put to bed. Unexpectedly she found herself with time to think.

The talks at camp were about the person and nature of Jesus Christ. Ruth had never heard this subject clearly presented before. She had drifted on with never a serious thought about who Christ really was. Now she was forced to think through the issues.

The debate raged within her for a time. Then the matter became crystal clear. A decision was made. Ruth accepted Christ as her personal Saviour, and gave herself there and then, unreservedly to him. It was a sudden, life-changing decision. For some, conversion comes slowly, as a step-by-

29

step process. Not so for Ruth. It was a decision which led to a radical rethink about her life. It was to take her to the ends of the earth and the limits of endurance for her Saviour's sake.

That day changed Ruth's life.

In October, Ruth began her medical training at Birmingham. The early days were traumatic. There was something appalling about the first few visits to the dissecting room, reeking with the acrid smell of formalin. To cut up dead bodies was gruesome – a far cry from the civilities of the sixth form. Gradually, Ruth found horror replaced by fascination, and that in turn replaced by unholy familiarity, spurred on by the threat of exams just around the corner.

Student life brought freedom. Certainly there were lectures and practicals to attend; certainly there was a great deal of reading to be done and knowledge absorbed. But time was one's own. Students were free to make new relationships, to put the world to rights over endless cups of coffee late into the night. Free to think new thoughts. For some this was a heady mixture, for others frightening. Societies abounded, each competing for allegiance (and money), providing scope for learning new, or developing old, interests. It was a great period of life, but in many ways totally divorced from the real world outside.

Ruth thrived on all this. Her desire and determination to become a doctor made sure she did enough work. Her climbing interests were nurtured in the Mountaineering Club. Her new-found faith matured and blossomed under the influence of the Christian Union. The emphasis on personal commitment to the living Christ, and the supreme authority of the Scriptures gave Ruth a solid grounding in the basic tenets of her faith. She learned there, too, the value of the daily time alone with her Lord, studying the Bible and in prayer. In the struggles to come, it was these times which enabled her to hold firmly to her faith when tempted to give up, and which gave her the strength to go on.

One enormous change met with at university, especially for young people from the typical public or single-sex grammar school of that period, was the sudden exposure to members of the opposite sex. Ruth had several passing boy-friends, and formed a deeper relationship with an older medical student who was also in the Christian Union. Years later, she recalled her mixed motives in attending Bible study groups which he was leading. She remembered one particular study about 'Guidance' which he had led, very helpfully; but she reckoned that subject under those circumstances, was more than a little hazardous!

The relationship resulted in lasting friendship rather than marriage and they maintained contact throughout the years ahead. Ruth never formed another close attachment, but she did not appear to have the problems many of her later colleagues had in accepting the single life. She would very much have liked to be married, but she accepted her singleness as from God, and gave herself totally to the service of others.

# 5
# DECISIONS

Ruth was always an ambitious person. She remained ambitious throughout her life, constantly striving for new heights in herself and her work. At that stage in her Christian life, however, her ambitions needed to be channelled.

> Soon after I became a Christian, I had a feeling that the Lord was to ask me to be a missionary. I was a Christian, but a missionary was the last thing on earth I wanted to be.

She felt missionaries were strange characters with hair in buns, altogether uninteresting creatures who carried big Bibles.

Like many missionaries Ruth began by resisting this 'inner call', and she occupied herself in her medical studies. From early days she began to develop a love for surgery, and later won a surgical prize. The hope stirred that she would one day become a top surgeon. Her boyfriend, leading a Bible study, had emphasised that circumstances could give an awareness of God's leading. Ruth was encouraged by that to press on in her aim to be a surgeon.

Then, suddenly, without any reason, she failed the next

exam. It was only by one mark, and she did not have to resit it.

> It was quite clear to me as soon as I saw the list of results – I knew the Lord wouldn't take 'no' for an answer, and that my direction lay elsewhere. So I said 'yes' and immediately came peace and the complete assurance that missionary medicine was the right way for me. That has never been shaken.

Once her mind was made up, Ruth was never one to hesitate, she rang her mother that night, with never a thought as to how her news would be received.

'I've failed my exams, but I'm going to the mission field.' The news was not well received!

Like many mothers before and since, Mrs Watson was very upset. It cost her a great deal to see her daughter heading overseas, a fact which never entered Ruth's head at the time. She felt she was losing a daughter – for all she knew, to die of some dreadful disease in a hostile land. The joy of seeing her daughter married, of playing with grandchildren, of weekend visits home, of holidays together – she was to be denied all this.

Her father didn't like the decision either – he was paying quite a sum to educate Ruth. He was agnostic at the time, and saw Ruth's training and ability as being completely wasted. He told Ruth, however, that her life was her own, and she must do as she would with it.

Her parents contacted the surgeon with whom Ruth was working at the time, and enlisted his help. He tried everything to dissuade her, including offering her extra money to stay on as his assistant. She had fibrositis of the shoulder, and as he was injecting it one evening he said, 'I hope this stops you going off abroad.'

Ruth Watson was not so easily dissuaded. Once her mind was clear, she headed straight for her target. It was this single-minded, positive approach which, above all, qualified her for pioneering work of the toughest kind.

Having decided to be a medical missionary, the next question was 'Where?'. Two years passed, and the question remained unanswered. Finals were near. Ruth went to a student missionary conference with the theme 'Guidance'. The roots of the Inter-Varsity Missionary Fellowship lay back in the 1870s, growing out of the 'Cambridge Seven' who scandalised the Victorian world by giving up their wealth, positions (including, for one, the captaincy of England's cricket team) and titles to go to China as missionaries with the newly-formed China Inland Mission.

Typically, it wasn't the conference theme which provided Ruth with the answer, but a casual conversation. 'What about Nepal?' she was asked, out of the blue. Ruth had not even considered such a possibility. But she had inherited her love of mountains from her father, and that, plus the enquiry, was enough to form a complete picture of the direction she was to take.

'It was all quite casual, no hours on my knees worrying over it, no flashing words, just a total certainty. That was it. I've never had a moment's doubt since that Nepal was the place for me,' Ruth recalled.

God guides in many different ways, taking into account our personalities. Our responses are different. Some spend months, even years agonising over such momentous decisions and at the end of it all step out in timorous faith. Not Ruth. Direct and positive as usual she knew and that was that.

Twenty-five years later, as Ruth did a ward round in the Shining Hospital, an old lady patient told Ruth that she wasn't sure about what happened after death. 'But I know,' said Ruth, about to go on and explain the Christian's great hope. 'Yes,' interrupted the old lady, 'you would!'

In the summer of 1949 Ruth Watson qualified. She had a clear aim in mind as she entered her house jobs: to be as well prepared as possible for her work in Nepal.

House jobs then were hard, even harder than today. It was supposed to be a privilege to work under the 'Great Consultant', trailing round after him, leaping at his every command. Pay was appalling, living conditions bad, and time off almost non-existent. Yet that period of training was vital to the building of a doctor.

Ruth's time at the famous Birmingham Accident Hospital was of special benefit, and she learnt skills there which were to enable her to become as skilled a surgeon as any.

Those were hard days, walking through the mists of tiredness. The comradeship, often hilarious, in the doctors' mess was vital. Britain was still living in the period of ration books and poor meals, and extra food for the long night hours was much sought after. It was known that the hospital Matron had a closely guarded store room full of goodies, including gifts from relatives to patients quite unable to make use of them. At any rate, junior doctors regarded them as fair game and Ruth, being the smallest, was appointed chief forager. While Matron was at dinner, Ruth would crawl under her window, through the store room door and remove some of the excess gifts. All in a good cause she argued. She was never caught.

All this time, Ruth sought to find out more about Nepal. The first thing she discovered was that there was no missionary work in Nepal. That was very confusing. Nevertheless, she was so sure that this was God's plan for her that she applied to a missionary training college, and was accepted.

She hated it.

From being a respected, responsible doctor, wearing whatever she chose, inevitably living a chaotic life centred on work, food and bed, she now found she had to conform. She felt restricted, pressed into a mould, and she resented it. In those days, deeply ingrained traditions at the college required the students to wear stiff, starched collars and cuffs. It was not felt glorifying to God to have your prayer time without these being firmly in place! Mattresses had to be turned twice a week and lisle stockings worn. To the modern, liberated Ruth, these rules were very galling. Some of the rules she later understood but others always made her laugh.

As part of their training, the students had to do home visitation. Ruth, complete with hat and starched cuffs, called at one house. The door opened. 'Oh, hallo, nurse, called to do the enema then?' said the owner. Dr Ruth was not amused!

Many things were enjoyable, however. She learned much about mission history, more about the Scriptures, and there were many practical lessons in cooking, gardening, sewing and other topics. There was time too, to be sure of God's call. Ruth was challenged on this by the Principal and others who felt she should have a specific 'word from the Lord', some verse of Scripture which indicated her calling. She read and read in search of more specific words, but none came, except a reference to 'Seven steps' in Ezekiel chapter 40, which she took to be the seven years of preparation she had between starting medicine and going to the mission field. The way in which God had spoken to Ruth might not have fitted the conventional thinking of the day – but for her it was clear and compelling.

Hard though this college training was, it proved vital for Ruth. She needed to learn humility, respect for others and dependence on God. Learning to live closely with other, very different, people was important. So too was learning to accept things she couldn't understand. It was only when she arrived in Nepal and went through the traumas of those first five years that she understood what her year at college was all about. Without it she would undoubtedly have had a major row and returned home.

During the year at college she met Dr Pat O'Hanlon. It was likely that Nepal would shortly be open to missionary activity following the political upheavals there, and Pat O'Hanlon and Hilda Steele were home briefly to look for new workers.

Pat told Ruth about the start of the mission as she and Hilda sat on the Nepal border in June 1934, whilst trekking in the Darjeeling area. Up at 12,000 feet, the air was clear, and Everest could be clearly seen in the distance. Clouds rose, covering the mountain. And God spoke, clearly, silently, in their hearts. God's purpose for the land might be obscured, as clouds obscured the mountain, but his purpose remained, ready one day to be revealed.

Ruth now knew her future direction and applied to Miss Isabel Graham, Home Secretary of the Nepal Evangelistic Band. She was accepted as a suitable candidate.

So Ruth had decided that Nepal, and the NEB were for her. Pat O'Hanlon visited Ruth's parents, who were still far from happy. They told her of Ruth's attacks of rheumatic fever, and were reassured when told that she needed a medical examination and, if she were not fit, would not be finally accepted. The medical, however, confirmed her fitness. Ruth's way to Nepal was clear.

Her training finished, the final preparations lay ahead. There was much to do. People to see, letters to write, shopping to be done. Trying to shop for the next five years, even in those days of relative shortage, was an exercise to stretch the mind as well as the pocket. Trunks to pack and send. A constant mixture of excitement, anticipation, apprehension. Tickets arrived; the itinerary was planned. Then the final twenty-four hours. The last morning, the last lunch. Panic shopping. The final pack, trying to fit everything in. Then tidying up. The last evening together, wondering when, if ever, they would all be together again. Fitful sleep. Most missionaries know the experience, and it is never pleasant. The hardest part — the final goodbyes — was yet to come. It *was* hard and the passing years never made it any easier.

So Ruth boarded her boat train at Liverpool Street, bound for Tilbury and the SS Chusan. Choked with emotion, holding back tears, she waved out of the window, then thankfully collapsed in her seat, suddenly drained.

Not for long. Soon her mind was looking forward, leaping ahead to what lay in front.

Behind, on the station, her sister Jill found loving arms leading her away, comforting and encouraging. For Jill, too, that was quite a day. She later caught another train in a different direction, bound for Cambridge and her first teaching post. For her, there was no glamour, no pedestal, just the ordinary business of starting life's work. Not for Jill the drama of the Himalayas and an unknown land. Nevertheless, that was the first step of several which ended with her choosing to teach in the East End of London, as hard a mission field as ever Nepal would be. She eventually became head in a junior school in the vast newly created high-rise suburb of Tower Hamlets, where social problems were common. She loved it.

Back at home, supporting each other, were Dr and Mrs Watson. They had said their goodbyes the night before Ruth's departure. For them there was no excitement, no glory. Just an aching, empty void.

# 6
# SETTLING IN

A few weeks later, at the other side of the world, Ruth awoke to see sunrise over the Himalayas, the beginning of the fulfilment of her dream.

The last morning of the trek – and Ruth and her friends stood awestruck on the high ridge which seemed like the roof of the world. They watched the sun's rays strike first one then another mighty peak as daylight spread from east to west along a hundred miles of mountains. Towering above the Pokhara Valley, dominating the whole scene, was Fishtail Mountain. This 23,000 foot conical peak rose sharply out of the valley floor, one of the most perfect of earth's mountains, believed to be the home of the gods by the local people. Man has never set foot on its summit.

They descended towards the valley floor. As they went, another sight caught their eye – an aircraft landing on the Pokhara airstrip. Aircraft had just started flying, irregularly, to Pokhara, and that old DC3 had two people on board who were to be vital to the newly arrived group.

Having reached the small town, the first task was to find

somewhere to stay whilst looking around. Pat and Hilda knew of a government guest house.

'You must get permission from the Governor first,' they were told. 'He's just come over on the plane for a day's fishing.'

Permission was sought and given, but any thoughts of comfort were quickly dashed. Ruth was distinctly unimpressed. There was not one stick of furniture. The floors were made of rough planks with gaps of more than an inch between them. Cooking had to be done in the open and tents needed to be erected for toilets. Water was half a mile away and, as usual, they had a constant audience. Ruth, from her background of middle-class comforts, was beginning to feel the pressure. They paid off the porters – giving more than they had planned because of the size of the party and the extended trek. They were almost penniless, but at least they had a roof – of sorts. They could collect themselves and plan for the future.

The following morning they were surprised to have a visitor. An American tourist had arrived on that plane the previous day and was about to return. He had packages from the Summerhayes.

'They asked me to deliver these if I could find you. If not, I was to take them back,' he explained.

Gifts and money. Perfect timing – God's timing. Had they arrived in Pokhara one day later, they would have missed these vital gifts.

Ruth and her colleagues set about exploring the Pokhara valley. It is smaller than the other significant valley of the interior, Kathmandu. The valley, ringed by hills, is 3,000 ft above sea level, its climate, though kinder than the heat of the plains, is often violent. To the north lies Annapurna with its four peaks, forming a gigantic semi-circle around Fishtail, whose foothills formed the northern boundary of the valley.

The river Sheti (meaning 'white') flows through the valley from the glacier on Fishtail. It is a holy river, and flows sometimes slow and wide across sands formed from mica, sometimes crashing through gorges 300 feet deep and 20 feet wide. Particularly beautiful are the three lakes. Around one of these, close to the town, and excellent for swimming, the tourist industry later developed. The other two are smaller and more remote.

The new arrivals were learning to live together.

Even during the trek there had been a tendency for groups to polarise: the older ladies who had worked together for years, planning and organising, and the younger group, one moment excited by the possibilities, the next thrown into despair by the size of the need and the smallness of the resources.

It is hard for us to grasp the situation in which these individuals found themselves. The experienced missionaries were very used to the ways of the British Raj in India when status as foreigners produced separation from the nationals. The small group of new, untried, idealistic missionaries were from a very different background and experience, and looked for a closer contact with the Nepalis as they settled in.

The Nepalis themselves had been isolated for so long that they knew nothing of colonialism. These Europeans were a totally unknown quantity, to be viewed with suspicion. Why had they come? What were they doing? A conversation between Nepali men was overheard: 'What are they, male or female?' one asked. 'Neither, they are memsahibs,' came the reply.

Problems were inevitable.

In Pokhara Ruth met Buddhi Sagar. Ten years previously, Buddhi Sagar had been living in Pokhara when a smallpox epidemic raged through the town. Buddhi's wife and all his children died. To die of smallpox was normally considered an honour for this was the only way in which the goddess of smallpox could be satisfied.

Buddhi was a high caste Brahmin who had often officiated at Hindu worship, at births, marriages and deaths. He was respected and honoured. He had suffered the death of an earlier family and after this second tragedy, honour was far from his mind. He felt the gods were against him.

'They had been cruel to me. I am no longer going to serve them,' he decided. 'I'll leave Pokhara and go to India. Perhaps Putali will go with me.'

He set off for the home of Putali, a nineteen-year-old Brahmin girl whose family lived in a village thirty miles from Pokhara. It was 1943.

Discussions with Putali's family revealed that the Japanese had spread from Burma into east Assam. Undaunted, he decided to head for Shillong, in the Assam hills. Next morning he managed to speak with Putali alone, and she agreed to elope with him. When everyone had gone to work in the fields, they left hurriedly, starting on the long journey to Assam.

There he met David Mukhia, a Nepali from Darjeeling and a Christian. David had worked with Dr Lily O'Hanlon in Nautanwa, and Buddhi knew Nautanwa from his journeyings. Drawn together by their common background they talked. Inevitably, talk turned to the subject nearest to David's heart — his God and Saviour. Buddhi, the disillusioned Brahmin, had an open mind, and quickly became serious in his quest for more understanding. Putali, by now the mother of a small child, was not so interested.

'Well, I'll never become a Christian,' she announced.

Buddhi believed and was baptised. Immediately he became an outcast. Two years later, following the death of her child, Putali believed, and together they determined to show their new faith to others. Where better to start than Nautanwa, for their faith meant they could not return to

Nepal? Whilst they were in Nautanwa, yet another child died of smallpox. But this time despair was replaced by hope.

So began a friendship with the missionaries which was to be vital to the establishing of a medical work in Pokhara, and to the establishing of the Christian church inside Nepal. The vision for Nepal belonged, if anything, more to the exiled Nepali Christians than to their European missionary counterparts.

Following the revolution in 1951, Buddhi was allowed to return home. With great difficulty he managed to reclaim some of his land. Once established, it was he who sent out the invitation to Pat and Hilda to come and work in Pokhara. When eventually the two got permission and visited Pokhara, he was able to show them around. They were convinced this was God's place for them and they walked the length and breadth of the town claiming it for God.

With the arrival of the whole group in Pokhara, the first problem to be solved was the need for a base from which to work. They searched for three days, and then Buddhi Sagar came up with a plan.

'Why not come to my land? You can build bamboo huts with thatched roofs and live there,' he suggested. 'It will only take a week to build, and even out of town at my place, people will crowd in for medicines.'

It seemed a good idea, and very shortly Ruth took her turn at digging out the foundations for the houses and the pits for the toilets.

On their first Sunday in Pokhara, worship was held on Buddhi's land. His family quickly became the focal point for the Nepali Christians and services were held regularly in his house. As the months passed, the house became too small as Nepali neighbours became interested in the Christian message, impressed by the change in Putali and in Buddhi. The church then met in the shade of the bamboo tree, but this also soon became inadequate. Soon Buddhi built a simple open-sided church with a white cross on its roof. Eighteen months later it was discovered that no churches were allowed in Nepal, but nobody complained and to this day, long after Buddhi's death, believers still worship on that site in an enlarged building. In 1970 David Mukhia, so influential in Buddhi's pilgrimage, returned in his old age as pastor.

The houses were built in eight days. They were a little basic perhaps, but adequate. There were only three huts, one for use as a dispensary, the other two divided into eating and sleeping areas. This was Ruth's first home in Nepal and it was good.

'It is still very much camp life,' wrote Ellen Meinke, who shared a room with Ruth, 'but every day it gets a bit more comfortable. Ruth has brought some very colourful checked material which divides our room from the communal living room. A stove has been made of stone and clay so we can cook indoors.' A gust of wind later blew the roof off the bathroom, 'so we look straight up to the stars when we are bathing. With a hoar frost on the ground outside, it is rather chilly!'

Despite limited facilities, there was no shortage of patients. The people had been used only to herbal remedies or witch-doctoring. They began to come in increasing numbers, stretching resources to their limit. The first mission hospital in Nepal began to function. Faith was becoming reality.

# 7
# THE SHINING HOSPITAL

Barely a week after they had moved into the new compound on Buddhi Sagar's land, there was a minor rebellion. A number of injured were brought in. Medicines had to be dug out from the bottom of trunks and basic treatment given. One evening a man was carried in with gunshot wounds to his leg. Gangrene had set in and he was in great danger of losing his life. An operation to amputate the leg was vital if his life was to be saved.

For the journey in, each member of the party had been restricted to three books — one medical, one religious, one fiction. Ruth had brought a book on surgery. Though instinctively she yearned to be a surgeon, she had received no formal training. Pat O'Hanlon had done no surgery for years. It was over to Ruth. Rummaging through the packing cases they found that most basic of surgical sets, a ship's surgeon's case, which had been given to her.

One of the thatch and bamboo huts was prepared as the operating theatre. The operating table was made from packing cases pushed together, with newspaper as a cover. To add to the problems, it was by now dark. The pressure lamp was found – but no paraffin. The medicinal brandy was tried instead, but refused to light. So torches had to be used. A cooking pot was boiled over an open fire and the instruments were sterilised in that. There were no gowns or caps or masks. The team put their white coats on, back to front, tore up some mosquito netting and used it to tie up their hair. Ruth studied the book – she had seen amputations as a houseman but had never done one. The book was woefully short on detail.

All was ready. Earnest prayer was made with the patient, seeking the help of the God and Father who had called them into this situation. Hilda Steele administered the chloroform. Ruth cleaned and began the surgery. Willing hands held torches. In time the leg was off. Amazingly, the patient survived and, when healed, returned home. His was the first of thousands of lives saved by the intuitive, careful skill of Ruth Watson. It was the first time modern surgery had ever been performed in the remote hills of Nepal.

From then on, no operation, however routine, would begin without prayer. The patient's permission was always sought, and never refused. It was explained that it was the custom to ask God for help and peace.

On one occasion a Tibetan man with a badly injured arm required several operations. Before the second operation he seemed much more anxious. Ruth and her colleagues tried to discover why, but he could speak no Nepali, and they no Tibetan. Eventually it was discovered that, during the first operation, they had held his hand and said something, which he thought must be magical. He was afraid they were doing it again. It took a long time to work out what he meant – time which was supposed to be spent operating. Eventually they managed to explain that they had prayed that God would give him peace in his heart.

'That's funny,' he replied, 'because when you did, that's just what happened.'

Whilst on the trek into Pokhara, Ruth had met a girl with an ugly, disfiguring scar on her face. Years earlier, three girls had been cutting grass for animals. (In the dry season, the animals' natural pasture dries up and girls are sent with their knives and baskets to search for grass or leaves. Often this means climbing trees or cliffs to find enough food.) At the end of the day, the three girls had an argument about which grass belonged to which girl. Their argument turned into a fight with their knives. One lost a hand, another her nose, and the third had been slashed down her cheek, giving her this scar which drew her eyelid down to her upper lip.

'Come to Pokhara in a month's time,' Ruth had said rashly. 'We'll deal with that for you.'

Ruth was fresh, raring to go, with no thought of the implications of what she had said.

The girl came, creating a minor problem, because it had been agreed that the conditions were not good for plastic surgery, and it should not be done. However, Ruth, who loved plastic surgery, was unhappy to break her promise and prevailed. The result was good, and the confidence of the local people grew.

Soon after came the first abdominal operation. The thought that one's abdomen could be opened was horrific to the people. The patient made them keep it a secret from her relatives until she was better, asking only her husband for consent.

The first thoughts of the newly arrived group were to try to establish the hospital on that site. It was not ideal, however, being too far from the bazaar. There was much opposition, too, from Buddhi Sagar's Hindu relatives and others in that Brahmin village. The mission group were 'unclean', and able therefore to contaminate the Brahmins' food and people. The Nepali Christians had broken caste, and were eating with members of other castes, something unheard of to the orthodox Hindu. The village was being 'defiled'. That people were being helped mattered not at all: ritual cleanness mattered much more. Jesus had frequently experienced this type of opposition – always from the religious.

The surrounding area was wild, with dense forest. Leopards lived in those forests, and could be heard roaring at night. One patient was brought in with leopard mauls. The staff were informed that these patients always died on the fourth day. Much prayer was made, and the wounds were cleaned. He survived, and went home, to the amazement of his village. He was the first in that village ever to survive a leopard attack. Fear alone often killed the victim.

Bears also roamed the wooded slopes. Rice harvest in November often found these black Himalayan bears coming out of the hills in search of food. Bear injuries are particularly appalling. Bears run faster than any man, and escape is impossible. They grab from behind, tearing at the face with their great claws, ripping skin and breaking bones. Years later, one Christmas Eve was spent attempting to repair the arms and face of one poor victim; a four-hour session, to the accompaniment of the carols sung by the choristers of King's College Chapel, Cambridge, received live on the BBC World Service.

The other danger was from snakes – Ruth's greatest fear. Wet weather brought them out. Only some, the krites, were poisonous, and it was rare for a person to die from a snake bite. Nevertheless, they could produce a bad injury and the group learned to go about with sticks in the wet weather, and to wear shoes instead of the more ususal thong sandals. The vibrations made by the heavier shoes scared the snakes away. Yet krites could still be found curled up round a hairbrush, or in the corner of a bathroom. On one occasion, when water failed to come out of the tap, investigation revealed a snake blocking the pipe.

One of the more attractive wild animals was the snake's

great enemy, the mongoose. This 'friend' kept the snakes down. Later on, when better established, the group discovered another far less beneficial habit of the mongoose. It also attacked chickens, biting them in the neck. On one occasion a whole cageful was destroyed.

In those early days on the edge of the Nepali jungle, leeches also were a great menace, initially tiny, abounding in the wet, these creatures latched painlessly on to legs and ankles, sucked blood, swelled up to a great size and dropped off – all painless, but leaving the leg bleeding.

Jean Raddon and Ruth went out together on a maternity case one night. Ruth removed sixty-nine leeches from Jean, and both of them suffered a considerable loss of blood.

A new site was necessary. A letter home in January 1953 informed friends that already 150-200 patients came each day.

> By the end of a busy morning, we all had aching muscles, uniforms were dirty in an hour, and the dust kept us anxious. It is often late by the time the last patient has gone and the weary staff can begin to clear up.

A storm came, turning the hospital into a lake. Later a small cyclone swept down the valley. Some roofs were lost and a tent blown over a wall. These storms hardened their resolve to find a better site.

An ideal site was found on the old parade ground, a large flat area at the northern end of town. There was also a piece of land nearby which seemed ideal for housing, and the original buildings were dismantled and reassembled on this new site. Years later, they discovered that the Nepalis regarded the plot as haunted, the domain of spirits. The cremation site beside the river was just below the compound and few Nepalis would go there.

The living conditions were still very basic. There were

three huts for sleeping, two people per hut, and another for a dining room. An old stone house on the site served as a kitchen. Over the years these huts were added to and improved, and this compound still provides an attractive headquarters for the mission.

Huts were also erected on the parade ground site, only to be blown away in the first of the many pre-monsoon storms. Pokhara has a violent climate during the six hot months, with frightening winds, lashing torrential storms on many afternoons, and thunder and lightning as only experienced in a tropical storm. Hailstones up to two inches in diameter can shatter a crop in minutes, and people are regularly killed either by hail or by lightning. During the three months of monsoon 175 inches of rain fall, mainly at night.

Permanent buildings, requiring foundations, were not permitted on rented land. Prefabricated aluminium units were eventually ordered from Calcutta and flown in, to be erected on a base of rock quarried from local hillsides. The missionaries, and their visitors, Sir Christopher and Lady Summerhayes, all joined in the hard work preparing the base. 'Long Tom' was 30 feet by 20 feet, made of aluminium bolted on to a steel frame. This was used for outpatients. 'Twin block' was square, divided into four rooms, each 10 feet by 10 feet. This was the accommodation for inpatients, maternity or surgical cases. The following year, three more units arrived.

Dogs growled and barked as they saw their reflection in the new aluminium. Buffaloes lowered their heads threateningly. Friendly villagers were invited to see themselves in the Pokhara 'hall of mirrors', dissolving in laughter as they caught sight of their own reflections.

One day a group of women sauntered into the hospital. They lived in a village on a hillside around the valley.

'Can you see the hospital from your village?' they were asked.

'Oh yes. We often sit outside and look down on the house

that shines,' they replied, 'so we decided to come and see for ourselves.'

Thus started the Shining Hospital, cramped, inadequate and grossly overworked. Among the second batch of huts to arrive was another 'Twin hut', which served as the operating theatre. News came that the new King of Nepal was planning a visit to Pokhara. No king had ever come before – though one had tried and been repulsed! The missionaries were asked if they wished to be presented to the king. They were delighted, and asked if he could open the new 'theatre block', and then have tea.

'Yes,' came the reply, 'but you must wear hats, gloves and long stockings.'

This meant an urgent visit to India to borrow the gloves. On the day itself the tea was laid out – table cloths, best china and all – under a large tree. The king duly arrived, formal introductions were made, the red ribbon cut and the tour of inspection made. The sight of their king then sitting down to eat with the Westerners made a powerful impact. It earned the missionaries new status and new respect.

The Shining Hospital was established. The aluminium huts were intended to be temporary, but thirty years later they still stand, as heavily used as ever. The shine has gone, the walls are pitted by enormous hailstones. Cold in the winter, hot in the summer, yet able to withstand the storms and the monsoon, they proved a superb buy – easy to clean and simple to maintain.

This was Ruth's base for twenty-four years. All the staff had their uniquely valuable contributions to make. Ruth brought the vision, the drive, the charisma, which established the hospital as a place of compassion, love and dedication to a people in great need. She made it an example of how much can be achieved with very little.

# 8
# TENSIONS

In the early years there were tremendous pressures on the small group of pioneers. There were, on the one hand, the experienced, older missionaries who had been in India for many years and, on the other, the younger members of the group, new to Asia, unused to its culture and customs.

India had, of course, been part of the British Empire for many years. Beautiful 'hill stations' had been built in the Himalayan foothills, away from the dust and heat of the plains. The white man retreated to the cool slopes of Darjeeling, Nainital, Simla, Mussoorie and their like in the summer months.

The founder members of the Nepal Evangelistic Band left the dreadful heat, dirt and disease of the railhead town on the border each summer. They made the long journey eastwards to the town of Shillong high up in the relative cool of the beautiful hills of Assam. There they worked with Christian Nepalis, returning to the plains in the autumn. Throughout the second world war they stayed in India and, in many ways, the war passed them by. They were inevitably out of touch with the experience and ideas of the young women who came out to join them from post-war Britain. These young women had emerged from the struggles of studying and qualifying amidst the upheaval and disruption of Britain at war. Their attitudes and ideals had been deeply affected.

Britain was counting the cost of victory. For six long years all resources had gone into the war effort. Now came the time to rebuild – new schools, hospitals, houses and roads. Time to clear the debris, to reorientate shattered lives. Austerity was the order of the day, and rationing continued for several years. Out of this came Ruth and Joan Short and Jean Raddon, full of new hope, new ideas, new energy. The contrast between Pat and Hilda, and these three, was very great. The wonder is not that there were problems, but that these two very different generations were able to work so effectively together.

Nepal proved quite a shock. India had a good network of roads and trains ran across the plains and up into the hills. The hill stations were highly developed and very comfortable. A wide range of good food was available. Trekking was possible even in the monsoons and government rest houses and Dak bungalows were available for the traveller to stay in.

Not so Nepal. Only Kathmandu had roads and electricity. Elsewhere conditions were primitive. Travel was almost entirely on foot. Accommodation was available only in local houses, often on a mat on the verandah. There were no toilets or taps. There was no privacy. Food consisted of rice and lentils, with a few root vegetables or spinach in season. Meat was rare, and usually tough. Eggs were hard to come by.

Entering Nepal, even for the older, experienced missionaries, was harder than they had expected, and the newcomers found the going very tough. Inexperienced and idealistic, they had to make major adjustments. Many of the pressures were inescapable – crowds, noise, disease, poverty, poor diet, lack of privacy, lack of comforts. Today in Nepal, these things remain a problem to the new worker; much more so in 1952.

Even more difficult, and very subtle, were the adjustments these strong-minded, determined women had to make to each other.

During her first year in Nepal Ruth suffered a series of stomach disorders. The problem began with a bout of amoebic dysentry, the scourge of travellers to this magnificent but dirty land. Gradually Ruth developed colitis, which went on day after day; she was free from diarrhoea for only five days in her first year. She recognised, reluctantly, that the problem was in part at least psychological – a conclusion which deeply hurt her pride. She had thought that only inadequate and immature people experienced such problems. But they were the physical manifestation of the inner tensions she was feeling.

One of her colleagues suffered from palpitations which did not respond to treatment, and resulted in her being sent home early. As soon as she set foot on the boat for home the palpitations disappeared, never to return. She threw her medicine out through the porthole.

Attempts were also made to send Ruth home during that year because of her chronic ill health. Hard-headed, and determined, she retorted, 'God sent me here and I'm not going home until he sends me!'

Immediately before leaving England, Ruth had spent a very trying year at missionary training college. Having arrived in Nepal, she found that her trials were by no means over. Yet it was many years before they were spoken about. Letters home made no mention of the problems. The Home Council of the mission had no idea of the rising pressures. In those days one did not admit to problems – that would have been a mark of weakness and, as E D Hoste, successor to Hudson

Taylor, the founder of the China Inland Mission, pointed out, might shake public confidence.

It was more than a year before Ruth could bring herself to write even a general letter to her supporters at home; even then she made no reference to her difficulties and heartaches.

Later, Ruth was able to express the feelings she had kept to herself for so long:

> I went out with a very young mission which consisted mainly of older people, who often had not been home on furlough for many years, and had not kept up with modern thought. They had been brought up in the age of 'You do what you are told and that's that!' There was no explanation of decisions taken. For the first two years you were not expected to open your mouth. The forces brought against us were nigh unbearable.

Ruth's ideas and methods of medical treatment were sometimes a cause of contention.

On one occasion a colleague broke her wrist. Ruth felt it best that she went over to Kathmandu on the plane to have it X-rayed and properly set. She was told, 'If you can't set a fracture without an X-ray you are not worthy to be a doctor.'

It was not considered proper for a young woman doctor to have any contact with the male patients. 'Men would come in agonies,' she recalled, 'and I knew I could help them, but it was just not allowed.' Sometimes she treated them, in fear and trembling, when no one was looking.

Ruth was a very junior doctor when she left Britain. She was inexperienced not only in 'local' medical situations but also in her overall knowledge. She was full of enthusiasm and not a little headstrong and there were practical problems which she found it hard to understand. She saw issues in black and white. Often she saw only the point of view of the patient who was asking for her help, and failed to relate this to the other problems the mission group faced and was therefore unable to look for the balanced answer.

One such problem was finance.

In those early days money was desperately short. Resources had to be used carefully. Staff allowances, wages for Nepalis, maintenance of buildings and equipment, and essential travel all had to be squeezed out of the takings from the hospital. Gifts from home came slowly and irregularly at first. The need for anaesthetics, operations, the length of time spent on an operation and drugs used in treatment, were all submitted to scrutiny, and Ruth found herself having to justify to the non-medics much of what she did as a doctor.

Hilda Steele had the difficult task of being the treasurer. She and Ruth disagreed on many matters yet she gained a close insight into Ruth.

> Circumstances were adverse and medical and other supplies and equipment were very inadequate. Ruth was overworked – we all were – and good food was scarce. The food was not suited to Ruth's digestion, yet her plucky determination to pull her weight and make the best of a bad job put heart into us all and made the difficulties less daunting. She made light of having to operate in a makeshift hut. One day I was giving the anaesthetic. Ruth looked at me over her mask with a sparkle in her eyes and said, 'Would the anaesthetist mind removing the foreign body from the incision!' A piece of the thatched roof had fallen straight into the wound!

Heroic or unduly major surgery was questioned for another reason too. There were fears, probably well grounded, that too many deaths would have an adverse effect on the morale and confidence of the local people. Even many years later one or two deaths in a ward would result in patients running away, leaving other beds empty the next day.

The senior missionaries realised that a hospital could easily dominate the life of the group. They were keen that it should not grow to take over the mission because they felt their task was as much to establish the gospel and the church in the land as to establish a medical work. Attendance at Sunday services, three miles away, was compulsory, as was attendance at prayer times. The medical and nursing staff were kept firmly in their place and even when emergencies occurred prayer meetings and Bible classes had to be given priority. More than once Ruth was driven to tears by being kept from an operation or other essential treatment while the staff finished their prayer time. Nobody actually died because of this but it seemed to Ruth to clash with her idea of a loving God. In later years, when she was in charge, Ruth unconsciously tended to stray in the opposite direction. If busy times such as general meetings of the mission clashed with extra medical work, she would work even harder.

Ruth never had any doubts, right to the end of her medical career, about where her priorities lay. The patient in front of her was top priority, the one in need, for whom everything possible should be done.

This was a source of disagreement many years later when Ruth, with extensive accumulated experience of curative medicine, was a senior missionary herself. Who is my patient? Is it the person asking for immediate help? Or is it the wider community which never comes, yet whose need of treatment and preventive medicine is still great?

In the 1950s curative medicine was the universal aim and Ruth was ideally suited in skill and motivation to fulfil it. Indeed, it is impossible to establish effective preventive medical care without first winning the confidence of the community by effective curative medicine. Years afterwards, the first TB survey in Pokhara was a success because of the foundation of confidence laid by the early results in curing sick patients. Because they trusted Ruth, the people were prepared to accept injections from her colleagues to prevent a disease which they did not have.

These things were amongst the abundant fruit that was to come from the resolution of those early struggles.

For Ruth, however, with no inkling of how worthwhile it would eventually prove, the horizon was filled with the unreasonableness and frustration of the restrictions imposed upon her.

'I was not allowed to do the necessary antenatal care for one of the missionary wives,' she said, 'because it was not regarded as suitable for a single woman to examine a married woman.'

'I was desperately homesick. I think for the whole of my first term, five and a quarter years, there was no way in which I could consider that I belonged as a doctor to the team working in Nepal. I couldn't understand one jot or tittle of these awful things – and I still don't,' she wrote twenty years afterwards. 'I could never have survived without that initial training at missionary college.'

Ruth and the others kept silent, praying for a change. A brief respite came after her first monsoon in Nepal, when she was sent to Patna, to the hospital run there by the Zenana Bible and Medical Mission (which later became the Bible and Medical Missionary Fellowship – BMMF).

Dr Winifred Anderson was leading the medical work there and the friendship which began then between her and Ruth continued through the years, providing Ruth with much encouragement in a later protracted illness.

In Patna Ruth gained experience previously lacking in gynaecology and midwifery, disciplines in which she was later to excel in the Shining Hospital.

'Ruth was thin and bright when she arrived,' Win Anderson recalled, 'full of energy and enthusiasm, wanting to do surgery whenever she could. One thing stood out. She was always ready to take responsibility – indeed she tended to take on too much. One time she went ahead when she should have waited, and things went wrong because of her inexperience. She was very distressed, but had learnt an important lesson.'

Whilst in Patna, Ruth was joined by Eileen Lodge, a nurse newly arrived from England, and gaining experience on the way to Pokhara. They travelled to Pokhara together, Ruth feeling much refreshed for her time of freedom from stress and strain. She was now able to write her first general letter home.

Back in Pokhara, she and Eileen shared a new thatched mud hut which they named 'Swiss Cottage', not after the mountains in Switzerland, but the tube station in London!

Inevitably, because of the financial difficulties, when a doctor or surgeon wished to order a new drug or expensive piece of surgical apparatus this would be questioned. Often the proposed expenditure had to be shelved. Sometimes, however, these economies were taken to exaggerated lengths, as when harmless but ineffective drugs were bought rather than the more active and scientifically better drugs, so as to avoid any danger of side effects. In vain did the doctors explain that they were trained to detect and avoid these very side effects. It was apparent that there often was merely a clash of personalities rather than any genuine discussion of the rights and wrongs of any particular issue.

Ruth's feelings on the matter emerge in this comment:

> This appalling generation gap gradually became intolerable. Our medicine was primitive and the care we could offer was limited, but I know that people died who needn't have died. Medicines, including intravenous fluids, were sometimes hidden away.

Twelve bottles of intravenous fluids would have used up the whole month's budget for medicines. Ruth, fresh from a British hospital, found this terribly frustrating. The process of learning to make do, at which she was to become expert, was just beginning.

As the mission began to grow with the arrival of new recruits, so the financial situation grew worse. Each knew that there was no guaranteed allowance – there is none to this day. They shared what came in, and they shared their shortages.

On one occasion a new arrival, Dr Gerald Turner, had a bad toothache, and as there was no dentist in Kathmandu, he was hoping to go to Lucknow to the nearest one. There was little cash in the hospital. One day a gift of about five hundred rupees arrived and Hilda Steele, who was treasurer, gave him the lot and sent him off to Lucknow, leaving them with very little in Pokhara. They were learning to look to God and not man for their provisions – a faith mission at work in a situation as difficult as can be imagined.

Jean Raddon kept a diary:

> Our financial situation is very serious. There is little money and hardly any food, No shoes to wear, only my best sandals; I think the new families have nothing left to eat; a letter arrived from UK today, saying there was no money to send.

That particularly bad spell saw the missionaries with no allowances, living on gifts of eggs and vegetables given by patients in lieu of payment for treatment.

During this time one of the recently arrived children said grace one day, adding 'And send us some chocolate, dear God.' Poor parents! They tried to explain why God wouldn't answer that prayer just then. But God did! Next day a passing tourist handed the boy a gift – a small bar of chocolate. Their faith was stretched but God never left them destitute. Ruth's faith grew on this treatment, was tempered in the fire and became more resilient.

At the lowest point, when the strongest faith was tempted to despair, British soldiers, serving in Pokhara, presented missionaries with some left-overs – thirty-six boxes of rations!

Butter, meat, cheese, chocolate, coffee, sweets and even jam. The mail arrived. Money came over from Kathmandu. The siege was over.

The small Home Council in the UK now realised that with the growth of the mission the missionaries were not receiving adequate financial support. It was agreed that those praying for the missionaries should be told the situation. Supporters responded and as a result, allowances, along with personal gifts, became adequate.

The work expanded and developed remarkably during those first, tense, five years.

Following an outbreak of smallpox in a village near Pokhara, the local leaders invited the mission to vaccinate the population. Ruth and Jean Raddon went, vaccinating four thousand people. Unknown to them, the head man collected money from each person vaccinated, presenting sacks of coins to the missionaries! The two thousand rupees were used to buy more buildings for the hospital. They were flown in free from Calcutta. These pilots were most kind, often bringing gifts of fresh fish or meat. They would fly low over the compound, dipping their wings to show they had something, or someone, on board for the group. Messengers would then be despatched six miles to the landing strip.

The church too began to grow. The Nepali Christians took the message of Jesus to people totally ignorant of anything but their animistic form of Hinduism. The church, Nepali-led from the beginning, and with no denominations, began to be established. Regular services were held and the first group of twelve believers was baptised, amidst great joy.

As Ruth's first term in Nepal drew to a close, the tensions which had troubled her so much came to a head. There were increasing personal differences between the newer missionaries and the older ones, leading to much unhappiness, deep heart-searching and prayer, and eventually to confrontation and open discussion of the problems. Some even reached the point of writing letters of resignation, but Ruth did not, because her furlough was approaching and she wanted time to think. She did feel the time had come to speak out, however.

Hilda Steele recalls that time:

> I remember a walk alone with Ruth. She pulled no punches and told me what it cost her not to be able to give the best treatment to each of her patients, how bitter to her personal pride it was to be content with a second best result because of lack of facilities and supplies. I began to realise how much sacrifice there was for Ruth, a clever surgeon, in choosing a pioneer situation in which to serve. I also noticed how cheerfully she coped with what irked her, not showing the discontent or bitterness she felt.

Hilda was unwell, and it was hard for her to accept that the 'divinely planned programme leading to the fulfilment of God's purposes' had become out of date in the new and changing circumstances.

Soon afterwards, Hilda returned home to nurse a sick mother and sister and to convalesce. She eventually left the mission, but returned to a nearby isolated village where her drive and talents bore great fruit, establishing a dispensary and seeing a vigorous young church emerge.

For Ruth there was no immediate resolution of the problem, but the situation had been defused. Eventually action between the Field and Home Councils resolved the difficulties.

Ruth learned much from these sacrifices, even though she was terribly upset at the time. Reconciliation with Hilda was later complete, though to the end of her life Ruth failed to understand why these things had to be. She gained a depth of knowledge of herself and of missionary stress which proved of great benefit when she in turn became a 'senior missionary'.

There were touches of humour in the midst of the stress. Before she went on furlough Ruth visited Kathmandu for the first time. For five years she hadn't really looked at herself in a mirror. 'I got such a shock', she said. 'I'd got a great missionary bun – the one thing I'd said I'd never have! I went straight to a friend and said "Come on, cut it off!" She cut it off, saying she had never enjoyed anything so much in all her life. Oh dear, I got into trouble when I got back to Pokhara. I was the first to dare to do such a thing.'

So Ruth's first term as a medical missionary came to an end. Much had been achieved in those years.

She left for Bombay and the ship home, deeply weary from the experience, desperately needing her first leave. The tensions which had threatened the group were being resolved. The mission had grown, the hospital was established, and the church was beginning to spread to other areas of the land.

# 9
# FAMILIES AND FURLOUGH

Jesus started the controversy. Whilst addressing the crowd, he was told that his mother and brothers were outside wanting to speak to him. 'Who are my mother and brothers?' he asked, giving his own answer at once: 'Whoever does the will of my Father in heaven is my brother and sister and mother.'

His disciples, sent to the ends of the earth, had an identity crisis.

Ruth, leaving her nuclear family in the English Midlands, joined a spiritual family, the NEB, in Nepal. The members of the group were dependent on one another far more than was ever the case in Britain. There were discussions, debate, disagreements, dissensions. They studied and prayed together. They worked, ate, slept together. When money was short, as it usually was in those early days, they went short together, pooling their resources, having all things in common. They were so close, and so unable to move outside of their group for cultural and practical reasons, that it is a wonder they didn't have more problems. They were a family.

Small wonder then that Ruth, home on her first furlough after five and a quarter years, kept referring to her colleagues as her family and to Pokhara as her home. Her parents were deeply hurt.

Those early pioneers complicated matters still further. New to the culture, keen to learn how the Nepali family functioned, they sought relationships with Nepali families. For most, this was merely superficial. Not so for Ruth. She entered a *saini* relationship with Maya, a woman of her own age from the hill village of Bhajung, five hours walk from Pokhara. A *saini* is an unofficial 'adopted sister' relationship, carrying with it a deep responsibility, morally if not legally, to one another. It is common in Nepal, and respected.

Maya tells the story herself.

I was very ill with a pain in my chest. I went to the Shining Hospital to seek help there as an ordinary patient, and met Ruth. I did not get better quickly, and one day met an old Christian lady called Hannah. 'I had that problem' she said, 'and took lots of medicine, but it didn't help.' She had believed in Jesus, and soon after became really well. 'You believe in Jesus, child, and you will get better too.' I was amazed to hear this and decided to find out more about it. I found a Nepali woman who had a New Testament and bought it from her. The New Testament said, 'Repent, for the kingdom of heaven is at hand.' I just did that, believed in Jesus, and stopped worshipping idols and Hindu gods. And I was healed. I told others in the village about this, and some of them also believed in Jesus. There were about eight of us.

The next year I met Ruth on her way to another village, and stopped her on the road to tell her what had happened to me and the others. She showed me great love, and I began to spend time with her whenever I went to Pokhara. We talked about the Lord, and I was very encouraged and helped in my faith.

A year later Ruth said to me, 'Let's become *saini* sisters.' She gave me a cloth and I gave her a *jhola*[1]. With this ceremony we established our relationship. Our love deepened.

My *saini* came to the village and taught us, and the group grew.

When my mother died, my brother's wife threw me out because of my faith. Nobody would take me in, so I had to go to Pokhara. There I rented a room and started a cafe to earn my living. Ruth stood by me and encouraged me, sharing the word of God with me. I was greatly blessed through our love for one another. Later some Gurung[2] boys made much trouble for me, because I was a Christian, and the landlord, frightened that his house would be damaged, put me out.

I found a derelict house in a nearby village and stayed there. There were holes in the roof, and the rain poured in, making me very bitter. Ruth came, bringing an enormous piece of polythene, which completely covered the roof. She had the spiritual gift of understanding the problems which came my way.

Years later, I felt convicted that I had left my village. God wanted me back there. I shared this with Ruth, who took me to her room, laid hands on me and spoke in tongues. Then she told me what the message from God was. 'The Lord says, I have put my goodness and kindness upon you. Go.' She gave me a shawl and sent me off. When I arrived back in the village, amazingly the head man gave me a house to live in – I have been there ever since, serving God. The believers were delighted to see me back.

On one occasion when Ruth and I were walking up to the village a young Hindu holy man threw his shoe at Ruth and hit her. I was furious. Ruth picked up the shoe and very humbly called the boy over, and gave it to him. My *saini* always showed this kind of peaceful attitude and thoughts, and served everybody with great unselfishness.

My family really took to her, taking it in turns to have her in for meals. They called her sister, or auntie, never Memsahib! Those who were sick in the village were invited to the hospital, and sometimes she laid hands on them, praying for them, and they got better. She had the gifts of spiritual healing as well as medical training.

Later that year, the police came to Pokhara. There the

inspector asked me if I had obeyed the religion of Jesus. 'Yes,' I said, and so I was locked up for two weeks wth eleven others. Ruth sent me a *parti*[3] of puffed rice and three hard-boiled eggs. Eventually I was sentenced to a year in jail. When I went, I had only the clothes I stood up in. All I had were my two dogs. Because I followed the Christian faith, my dogs and I went to prison. A week later, my *saini* sent me a shawl, pillow, blouse, bedding, soap, a sari, a plate and cooking pots. In prison you have to cook for yourself with the rice they give you, and keep yourself clean. These gifts were gifts of love.

After finishing my sentence, I went back to the village, and we started worship services again. We also had a Christmas feast, and Ruth, as always, sent a small gift of money to encourage me.

Just as Jesus Christ had a quality which imparted peace, so too did my *saini*, the Kanchi Doctor.'

It was a long way from Maya and her village to the comfortable home of the suburban Midlands of England. Exhausted in mind, body and spirit from those formative, hectic, traumatic five years, Ruth left Pokhara for her first furlough. The boat trip was a mercy, giving time for some physical recovery, but the traumas of mind and weariness of spirit were not so quickly cured.

Ruth had written frequently to her family, and after that first year had produced regular news for her prayer supporters. The writings had been superficial, however; as we have seen she never shared the deep thoughts of her heart. The problems of the young group were barely known to the home staff of the mission, let alone to their families.

Ruth was never very close to her mother, and letters to her father, though warm, were of a more academic nature. Engrossed in her work, Ruth recalled later that she was insensitive to the needs of the parents she had 'deserted' for far-flung parts. Five years had passed. Ruth had changed and so had her family. They were subtle changes, and took a long time to understand.

The initial reunions, with mission home staff and then family, were sheer delight, but a great sense of unreality pervaded their relationships. Very soon, evidence of Ruth's deep weariness began to be apparent. Decision-making became impossible.

It was six months before I became able to make the simplest of decisions for myself – like having a second helping of food. The limitation of thought and decision that had been put around me had made me unable to make up my own mind, from fear and loss of confidence.

Most missionaries find 'furlough' difficult – and so do their families. Abroad, Ruth's role was well-defined. Her responsibilities were clear-cut. Life had a regular timetable. In contrast, 'furlough' seemed artificial. Blocks of time were allotted – to be spent on holiday with family, to be spent on deputation, taking meetings round the country, to be spent on refresher courses, to be spent packing.

Jill Watson recalls spending months, even years, preparing for Ruth's furloughs, getting the house and garden ready, outings planned, special meals arranged. So often there was a crowd of people, and it was hard to spend time together alone, relaxed, to be able to talk of personal matters. Having her sister up on a pedestal was a hindrance to Jill's own spiritual development. She often felt she was in Ruth's shadow, and was slow to realise her worth before God in her own right. If the time with the family presented problems the time of deputation, lasting about nine months, was even harder. Ruth was often away, sometimes for weeks on end. This was specially hard for her mother.

On the tapes made shortly before her death Ruth commented strongly on furlough times.

I was completely bowled over by everything. When we went shopping, I found I couldn't buy anything. There was so much choice. A colleague described going into a supermarket for the first time. She was utterly confused, couldn't find her way out, and heard a remote voice over the loudspeaker asking what she was looking for!

Everyone looked so well fed. Even the cows and sheep looked prosperous. And the dogs...!

I couldn't bear to see any waste, even a dripping tap. To be able to turn on a tap and drink the water was a forgotten luxury. All these things produced tensions because of a difference in attitude. I tended, like my colleagues, to become intolerant and self-righteous. 'Here's us suffering out there, going short, whilst they have been living it up over here.'

Most people returning from the developing world have similar reactions. Some can't face the realities and become silent, hiding away. Many find their priorities changed, sometimes permanently. All are affected in some way.

'Furlough should be a time for catching up, being re-integrated into western life again, 'Ruth commented. 'Time for settling back into the family, the local church, and into one's profession. The missionary should be taken off his pedestal, go into an ordinary job, and become a learner and normal human being again!'

If these tensions were there for Ruth, they were more strongly felt by her parents, who were still unable to understand why she had gone to Nepal. They could see, though, that deep down she was convinced of the rightness of that decision, and so were happier in their own minds.

The relationship between the mission and the parents of missionaries was given a lot of thought and comment by Ruth after her final return from Nepal.

Parents must be made to feel they count. The whole family

must be included in the fellowship of the mission, long before the person goes abroad. This is not easy where the parents are not Christians. Trust and understanding have got to be developed first, and a feeling that they are involved in all decisions. This is particularly so for the parents of the single girl.

She suggested that this was so important that a member of the mission home staff should be specifically appointed to forge this link, to keep in contact with parents while the missionary was abroad, sending literature, inviting them home to show photos or slides or just to talk.

The exclusive relationship which has traditionally developed between the mission board and the individual missionary must give way to a wider relationship involving the missionaries' families. This is even more important during furloughs when families expect a frequent, close relationship with their son or daughter. My parents would have loved to have been drawn in, but felt excluded.

Missionaries going off for the first time need to be counselled about these problems in relationships, so that they are able to cope with their parents' reactions.

For Ruth, returning home exhausted to the heroine's welcome was no help towards her recovery. She told her sister:

When you return, you are so often stuck up on a pedestal — 'wonderful missionary back from Nepal'. You give a talk, show some slides, tell a marvellous story. And everyone thinks you are marvellous, and mentally places you on a high, remote pedestal. In fact, there are so many pedestals I would like to knock down. You are put on one before you go — 'Here's this bright young Christian giving up her life to the Lord.' When you come back there is admiration for what you are doing, and it is not good. It is not good for the missionary, not good for their work, not good for the people saying these things, and not glorifying to God. But it is easy for the churches to seize the opportunity to have an interesting speaker, especially if accompanied by slides, with a story to tell. The reaction after the meeting is, 'Wasn't that wonderful? What a marvellous experience.' But there are not two breeds of Christians — the first class ones who go abroad as missionaries, and the second class ones who stay at home. Missionary work is not a glorious success story, but a day to day slog with the Lord! There are peaks, but most of the work is just a stolid walk with the Lord. You don't enter some rarified spiritual climate by just going as a missionary to Nepal. You remain the same person, but under more and more stress, so that the weak places are very soon revealed. Many have cracked under that stress, evidence of inadequacies in our selection procedures.

Ruth could not get away from her pedestal even in Nepal.

I became *the* doctor. I was their doctor and almost their god. I was almost worshipped at times, this was one of the things which saddened me most. But the Lord reminded me that they also worship the cow!

In the early years Ruth had no strong church base, a frequent problem for doctors, nurses and others whose training takes them away from home for long periods. In 1968 her parents retired to Chedworth in the Cotswolds. Relationships with them had grown closer over the years. They had come to share her deep faith and understood her call more clearly and actively supported her. Ruth's father made several gadgets to help leprosy patients, including a battery operated muscle stimulator to improve muscle power in damaged feet. He also designed surgical instruments for Ruth.

Her mother made a cake for Ruth each Christmas, Easter and birthday. She baked it in a biscuit tin, liberally laced it with brandy, filled the space in the top of the tin with other sweet luxuries and posted it. Despite the unreliability of the post, not one was lost and many colleagues, teetotallers included, loved those cakes!

Ruth's father looked after the vegetable garden, while Mrs Watson produced a constant display of flowers. Next to the gate was Dr Watson's workshop, separate from the house, and above it was a delightful three-roomed flat where Ruth lived when she was at home.

Ruth was rarely at home even on furlough but when she was she brought a breath of fresh air to the village, where she was remembered with great affection years after her death.

Ruth loved to spend time with the children in the village but she always treated them as equals and expected them to behave in an adult way. They responded to her because they were fascinated by her tales of Nepal. She often showed slides at the village school and the 'Ruth Watson Cup', which she presented to them, is still awarded once a year. In Chedworth, though accepted as a member of the community, Ruth was still seen as somehow 'different' and accorded special treatment. Consequently she was a little detached, even from her neighbours and friends. In contrast, when in Nepal, she was warm and affectionate and was often to be seen playing with the mission and Nepali children many of whom she had delivered.

Ruth was much respected in the church in Chedworth, which supported her while she was away and enjoyed the tapes she sent back. But she was never able to spend enough time there to develop deep relationships, as she was so frequently rushing off to speak at meetings all over Britain. Realising the weakness of her own church base, which pushed her back more to regard the mission as her foundation, Ruth developed strong views on this subject.

When a church has a missionary going from it, the group should take on not just the financial support and prayer support, but take them on as a whole person, or family. This is very demanding. It is vital that the church becomes really supportive, for difficult times lie ahead. The missionary must feel able to write home completely freely when problems arise. This kind of rapport cannot develop without active involvement over the months, ideally years, with that church. It will need to be a very loving group to bear these things faithfully.

It is clear that Ruth saw furlough as a difficult time. She longed to see changes in the way it was organised – changes which in many ways have now been realised. Ultimately, though, she loved her furlough. It was a great time, so good to be back. She always spent as much time as possible learning new techniques in surgery, and patching up some of the gaps in her training. Lunch was often missed to allow more time for learning new operations in orthopaedics and gynaecology, enabling her to take new skills back to Nepal. Careful observation of the plastic surgeon enable her to become as skilled as any.

Just before she returned home for that first furlough, Ruth overheard two women talking about her in outpatients.

'You are going away soon,' they said.

'Yes,' she replied.

'How long for?'

'About a year.'

'A year! Oh, what a terribly long time. You will come back won't you? Don't get married and stay there. Bring him back and you can have *your* babies here.'

## Notes

[1] Nepali woven shoulder bag
[2] Maya's own caste – a hill group originating in Tibet, noted for their toughness. One of the fighting castes.
[3] 1 gallon dry volume

# 10
# KANCHI DOCTOR

From that first furlough Ruth returned to the delightful weather of India in winter.

Nepal, however, was in a political ferment – the first ever general election was to be held. A new constitution was being prepared. For the first time, the Nepalese were to vote for their government.

Elections completed, democracy went to work – but not too well. Corruption was widespread, true government was suppressed and the country headed fast for a new crisis. King Mahendra, son of Tribhuvan, the founder of modern Nepal, stepped in, adjourned and dismissed parliament, arrested the leaders, and outlawed all political parties. In their place he introduced a unique system of government, which continues today with the blessing of the great majority of Nepalese, following a referendum in 1980 to reconfirm it.

The Panchayat system is a pyramidal system. Local people vote for local councillors. They in turn vote for district councillors who in turn vote from among themselves for zonal councillors. From among these, individuals are elected to the Rastriya Panchayat – the Parliament of Nepal, with 106 members. Most of these are elected, but the king has power to appoint also, and usually the prime minister has been a direct appointment (though he could equally well be an elected member). Thus the king is head of state and head of government. It is a system which has served Nepal well, giving a wide measure of stability and facilitating development.

Back in Pokhara, problems were being resolved and peace reigned. Ruth had broken with the tradition of long Western skirts and put on a sari, to the delight of the local people. She always wore the sari after that.

The local people called Ruth 'the Kanchi Doctor', to distinguish her from Pat, known as the 'Tuli Doctor'. *Tuli* is the name given to the eldest girl in a family, and the youngest is known as *Kanchi*. In between came *Maili* and *Saili*. People are rarely called by their given names in Nepal. They may be elder brother, younger brother, sister, old man or old woman. All old men are called *Barje*, meaning grandad. So Ruth was named 'Kanchi Doctor', and not only in Pokhara, but far afield, Kanchi Doctor became a living legend.

Ruth now had a male doctor to help her. Gerald Turner, with his wife, Lola, and family, arrived in 1958. For sixteen years Gerald was the quiet power behind the scenes, working very hard, doing all the administration, as both mission and hospital entered ten stable years of steady development. He was an excellent foil for Ruth, adding the stability which enabled her exuberant, extrovert love of work to abound, yet to be kept in check. Gerald was untrained in surgery, though for years he had to do lots of it. In his early years, he was expected to operate on the men. When the 'rules' changed, however, he was glad to give it up and leave it to Ruth.

Pat O'Hanlon did less and less medicine. Another male doctor arrived, Graham Scott-Brown. From a Harley Street background where his father became one of the most famous of ear, nose and throat surgeons, Graham could turn his hand to most aspects of medicine.

Under these three, the Shining Hospital grew and flourished.

By 1960, three afternoons each week were devoted to planned surgery, in addition to emergency work. The operating theatre was amazing. Two aluminium huts, joined like Siamese twins in the middle by a door, formed the 'suite'. One was the sterilising and laying-up room, the other the operating theatre, twelve feet by ten feet. There were two small ante-rooms. One acted as an instrument store, the other as the scrubbing-up area.

Nobody changed. Hands were washed with water tipped from a jug. The windows were without glass, covered with net curtains to keep out the flies, and enquiring eyes. The patient's relatives usually came into the theatre to see fair play, sitting on a sterilising drum in the corner, wearing outdoor clothes, frequently filthy. But if those relatives stood up to have a look. Ruth would let loose an icy tongue.

One nurse in theatre had the prime task of swatting any flies which strayed inside. Flies upset the Kanchi Doctor more than anything else. She was obsessional about them, believing that they were the greatest single cause of infection.

Operating conditions could be appalling. Light was provided from a very adequate large spotlight, but this was powered from the mains, which were grossly unreliable. All too frequently, the electricity failed in the middle of an operation, sometimes at a dangerous moment. Torches would be shone into deep holes whilst urgent messages were sent to Stanley Wall, the mission's maintenance engineer, to come and put on the hospital generator.

Heat was another major problem. They were operating inside huts. Surgery was always performed after lunch in the hottest time of the day. In the winter months this was fine, but in the eight hot months it was terrible. Heat radiated from the roof, sapping the energy, and inducing profuse sweating which brought its own problems. Somehow, Ruth didn't mind – though her colleagues did! Many discussions raged round this timing, but it seemed unchangeable. Latterly there was a fan, when the electricity worked.

Infection in the theatre was rare. The heat had something to do with that – no bacteria could survive the scorching heat of the theatre walls. Temperatures inside were up to 100°F. The walls were untouchable.

The main reason, though, was Ruth's devotion to detail. She trained her Nepali staff thoroughly – time and again standards would begin to slip and Ruth would drive herself and others to restore them. Sterile gowns, drapes, gloves and instruments were ensured. Perhaps the most important factor was her speed in operating. Sick patients were unable to stand prolonged surgery. Shortage of time, and her own temperament ensured minimum operating time. The rate of wound infections and complications was incredibly low.

Ruth's chief help in theatre was Regina. She had come, orphaned, from a village many miles away. Dr and Mrs Turner employed her initially as their cook. She had had no education, but learnt well. After a while she went up to the Shining Hospital to do her nurse's training. Many village girls with little formal education were accepted for training, giving them hope for useful employment, and Regina was one such. She did so well that, after her two year training, Ruth took her into theatre and trained her in sterilising, recognising instruments, laying up tables for surgery, cleaning away afterwards, and being the main assistant at most cases. Her help was invaluable. When it seemed the government might close the Shining Hospital, Regina, with others, began morning school (from 6 to 9 am) to increase her education, and, when she had attained a sufficient standard, she went off to begin government nursing training. The years of expertise she had gained counted for nothing. As with other girls, the Shining's loss was the government's gain.

If summer heat was the major problem, winter cold was another. The cold wind blew down off the Tibetan plateau at night. The windows were shut tight, but it was still rather cold for an emergency caesarian section, especially for the new baby. Dust storms were another problem, and so too was the occasional totally deafening hailstorm – one-inch hailstones bouncing off aluminium with thunder crashing around was the deafening accompaniment to some operations.

Ruth's range of surgery was enormous. In later years she was doing over six hundred major operations a year. She coped with all that came as best she could. Severe head injuries with brain tissues coming between the pieces of fractured skull, always seemed to come at night. Bear mauls, resulting in torn faces and arms literally in shreds, were horrid and took a very long time to repair. Many women, rendered incontinent as a result of difficult childbirth, were restored to normality.

On one horrific occasion a patient arrived with a gash in her neck and forceps hanging from it. A local compounder[1] had attempted to remove an enormous goitre and got into terrible trouble. The patient eventually fled to Ruth in a dire state. Ruth had no option. She got stuck into the mess and the patient survived.

Trouble always arose if the patient (usually a woman) needed blood. Relatives were terrified of giving blood, perhaps understandable in a primitive culture. Ruth would have none of it! She laid into the men folk, even threatened to discharge the patient. She had no time for their selfishness and many times, in that male-dominated country, verbally lashed men into submission. But if they were Brahmins, the problem was twice as bad. She stuck to her guns – and usually won. When taking blood, great care was taken to see the bottle was well hidden. One pint was all there ever was.

'Kanchi Doctor' was, par excellence, a plastic surgeon.

Burns were very common in the cold months. Nepali houses have a central fire, around which the family sit, and then sleep, for warmth. The children are put nearest to the fire. Many tragedies have occurred when a small child rolls into the fire in its sleep. Nepalis sleep so deeply, despite lying on hard floors, that it may be some time before the screams penetrate the consciousness of sleeping relatives. Others pull pots of boiling lentils or water over themselves. Women's saris get caught in the flames and blaze up.

Ruth evolved a very simple method of treating such injuries — vital in an overworked situation. Patients were cleaned daily with gentian violet, a purple antiseptic excellent for drying up burns. They were then put in the sun for two or three hours a day. After three weeks of this, they were ready for grafting. Sometimes on small children the area of burn was so great that there was not enough normal skin left to take for grafting on to the burnt areas. In these situations, the child's mother was taken first, anaesthetised as usual, and some of her skin removed. This skin was kept and, when the baby was on the operating table it was used as a temporary dressing on the burn until the child's skin being used for grafting had recovered enough to be used again.

It was even more difficult to straighten limbs and fingers long deformed as a result of burns. This often meant long, extensive and careful surgery, protecting vital nerves and arteries before being able to put on grafts. The lame were made to walk. Ruth personally looked after her skin-grafting blades, taking them to her room to sharpen them and care for them herself.

The Shining Hospital had its high days.

Apart from the visit of King Mahendra to open the operating theatre, Prince Philip also visited the hospital. He arrived early, before preparations had been completed, and was shown round by underprepared doctors. True to form, he not only wanted to see the tidy areas, but he also walked out to the back, near the toilets and the pits in which refuse was burnt. On another occasion Prince Charles, on a trekking holiday, also called in.

Royal visits also had their humorous side. The Queen of Nepal once arrived when no one was certain of her plans. Following lunch, walking up to the hospital eating an orange, Ruth heard a shout, 'She's here!' Unable to wash her hands, Ruth rushed up just in time to greet the Queen, apologising for her hands amidst loud laughter.

In 1961, Queen Elizabeth and the Duke of Edinburgh were dining at the King's Palace in Pokhara. The missionaries were presented. The previous evening Ruth had placed her white straw hat and gloves on her bedside table, only to discover in the morning, to her horror, that the rats had eaten part of the hat! She trimmed it neatly and wore it back to front so that her bun hid the nibbled remains. The dreaded missionary bun had its uses after all!

> Going home afterwards was quite enlightening. The people couldn't understand why the Duke was not the King! In England, the women must be most important, they thought. 'The mission hospital is run by women and here is their queen with a husband who is not a king!'

For the Nepalis life is desperately hard. Subsistence farmers, the majority of the population, are totally dependent on their crops. Planting time for maize and rice are critical. The planting, growing and harvesting of rice is an uncertain business and demands the attention of the whole family. The infirm or elderly stay at home to look after the small children and the house. Babies go with mothers, tied to their backs. Disputes arise, especially about stream water, which is shared between the fields, each person taking his turn. Frequently, attempts are made at night to divert the vital water from a neighbour's field, resulting in fights.

At that time of the year, from April to November, there is no time to be sick, even less time to go to hospital for treatment. Small wonder that patients arrive at the hospital late, in advanced stages of disease. Sometimes ignorance is the cause, often finance.

When informed that the sick person must stay in hospital for an operation or treatment, and that a relative must stay to feed and care for them (an absolute rule of the Shining Hospital), the relative faces a great dilemma. Who will look after his fields and his buffalo? Next year's food is at stake. Tragically, if the sick person is a child, especially a little girl, and sometimes if she is a woman, the family will take their chance and return home, preferring the death of one member to the starvation of all.

This was a situation Ruth understood, but could never accept. She was western-trained, hospital-orientated. Others, seeing this tragedy, would strive so to raise the general health of the community by vaccination programmes and health education that it occurred less often. Ruth was so swamped with the needy before her eyes that she had little energy left to think of such matters.

The Nepal government, latterly, has majored on this aspect of care, scattering health posts across the country at the expense of major hospitals. When the Shining Hospital started, these things were unheard of, and Ruth made little move to change things. Others tried with limited success, but were constantly sucked back into the spinning vortex of Shining Hospital activity. The Shining always had to be staffed, at the expense of smaller centres which were attempting what, in retrospect, was a more appropriate medical technology. In a country in which almost half the population dies before reaching the age of five, hospitals are not the answer.

Before she went to Nepal there was no time for Ruth to gain any practical experience in obstetrics. In the early years in Nepal, because of the restrictions placed on her by her colleagues, she did comparatively little. As the work developed, however, her deep love for the womenfolk resulted in more and more women coming for help. She spent furlough time in maternity units, and read the books. Her nursing colleagues knew a lot, and Ruth learnt from them and trusted their knowledge. Many years later, though thoroughly competent and widely experienced, she still did not feel at home in this subject, and when eventually Dr Mary Thomson arrived with a real love for obstetrics, Ruth stepped aside as quickly as possible.

Patients nearly always came late, though in latter years more of the bazaar women came for a planned delivery. In Nepali culture the woman in labour and for twelve days afterwards was regarded as unclean and untouchable. If things went wrong the relatives wouldn't consider coming for help until they were desperate. In the early days, Ruth and the midwives would go to the patient's home, sometimes involving a long, even overnight, journey. Often the patient was dead by the time they arrived, and eventually they insisted the patients must be brought to them.

These tragedies helped to break down barriers. Because of the strong caste system, it was impossible to enter a Brahmin home, though they could sit on the verandah outside. The midwives were regarded as defiled, because of the nature of their work. After a maternity case, the fee was paid by dropping the money into their hands, to avoid touching them. The missionaries, however, were allowed to deliver the baby, because an even stronger fear was at work, the fear that the mother would die with the baby still inside her. It was not love for the mother and baby, but fear which was the driving force. Should the mother die undelivered, the whole family would be cursed for generations. Ruth and her colleagues had the skill to get the baby out and free the family from that curse. Dying undelivered meant no funeral rites until the baby was separated from the mother. This cost the family a tremendous amount of money, because the person performing the dreadful deed on the corpse was himself cursed for three generations.

So maternity work grew on fear – a fear that was met by love and hope. 'Love does break down fear and cultural barriers and goes through to the people in need. Love is the only answer,' Ruth once said. Even twenty years later the problem still remained for these cultural and financial reasons.

Childbirth is a time of great danger for the Nepali women. Time and again tragedy strikes. A young woman, loved by her family, was carried for several days from a far village with obstructed labour. Within minutes of arriving and being seen, she died, too late to be helped. Other times women in their eighth or even tenth pregnancy came. Perhaps there was only one living child, and that a girl. Would this be the boy she needed? In the past, failure to produce a son and heir constituted grounds for divorce in Nepal.

The deep darkness and blindness in which some people live was often demonstrated. At the entrance to the Shining Hospital was a tea shop, providing snacks for the waiting patients. The owner's wife became pregnant. Attended by one of the traditional midwives she gave birth normally but complications followed. For three days she bled steadily. When finally the husband came over the wall in a panic, it was too late. She was carried fifteen yards from her house to the maternity room, and died before anything could be done. This darkness of spirit time and again brought tears and agonies to the staff.

Ruth and her colleagues battled not just against flesh and blood, ignorance and poverty; but against spiritual forces of darkness, blinding the minds of men and women.

Notes
[1] An unqualified medical practioner with limited knowledge and little training.

# 11
# WARFARE

Nepal is the world's only Hindu state. Hinduism has many millions of followers, mainly in the Indian sub-continent, although in recent years travel and disillusionment have led to many western young people turning to Hinduism and its close relative Buddhism.

The thought pattern of Hinduism has developed gradually over thousands of years, shaped by many races, cultures and religions. Indeed, the Hindu is perfectly happy to have a picture of the historic Christ and Muhammad up alongside the many-armed fantasy of Kali or Ganesh. He only becomes upset if it is suggested that Christ is greater than his other deities. He does not distinguish between fact and mythology.

Hinduism has developed multiple sacred writings, the Vedas, Puranas, Ramayana and Mahabharata being but a few. Indeed, the subject is so complicated that a whole university has been established in Benares, the Hindu holy place in India, to encourage study.

The concept of Brahma, the universal spirit, has appeared gradually. Brahma appears in different forms in different divinities – creator (Brahma), preserver (Vishnu) and destroyer

(Shiva). The wife of Shiva, the destroyer, is also seen in various guises — as Parvati (goddess of motherhood) and Durga (goddess of destruction). These contrasting natures represent the endless cycle from creation (birth), through destruction (death) to reincarnation (rebirth).

No summary of Hinduism can be adequate. There are many variations. The central thought is that though the body dies, the soul is reborn, maybe as a human, maybe as an animal. Every action influences the form in which the soul will be reborn in the next incarnation. Perfection may eventually be obtained, the soul entering salvation (*mukti*).

Small wonder, then, that many Nepalis regard the missionaries as working hard to save their own souls. That is not praiseworthy — only sensible. The gulf between Christianity and Hinduism is great.

The caste system, so strong in Nepal, has become absorbed into Hinduism, though it developed quite separately. It is forbidden for different castes to eat together. Rice is a holy meal, and even to look on the food of a high-caste person is to defile it. For this reason, most Nepalis turn their backs on others when eating. Education has hit the caste system hard, but in the villages it stands unchallenged. It developed from about 1,500 BC when the Aryans invaded India. They developed it to limit contact between themselves and the native Indian. The Brahmin caste today are of Aryan descent, the highest of the castes.

The caste system provides structure for society and division of labour. It ensures that all facets of community life are fulfilled, from the lofty priest to the lowly sweeper. Each keeps to his own area, giving stability to society — and to the individual who knows where he belongs. The low caste hopes for better luck next time round.

Just twenty miles from Nautanwa the small town of Lumbini lies on the plains, overshadowed by the massive foothills of the first of the Himalayan ranges. It was the birth place, in 563 BC, of a rich child of a warrior prince.

When he was twenty-nine, Siddartha Gautama was sitting under the Bo tree near his home. As he meditated, this young Hindu received four startling visions. As a result he left his wife and family, living a life of self-denial. This, however, brought him no peace. He spent more and more time meditating, and finally 'achieved enlightenment'. He was set free in his spirit, gathered others, as diciples, around him and sent them out to tell the world that the endless recycling of Hinduism could be broken and nirvana, a state of complete happiness and peace, could be attained.

This revivalist evangelist became known as the Buddha. Nepal was his home. Four main types of Buddhism have emerged. The Himalayan type (Mantrayana) believes in many saviours, revealed in and through the gurus (teachers). Disciples spend much time in sacred dance and meditation and reciting spells (mantras).

This is the religious background into which the Christian group came to work. Even a sketchy picture shows something of the enormous gulf which lies between the way the Nepali and the European thinks.

In practice, Pokhara had few orthodox Hindus, and even fewer Buddhists. These religions had become contaminated, as in all primitive cultures, by animism. People feared evil spirits. They had to be placated by animal sacrifices. A pigeon or chicken must be taken to the priest for minor problems, a buffalo or a goat for major matters. It was an evil, corrupt system which nobody dared to break — just in case. The lovable people visiting the Shining Hospital were often crippled by fear.

Most rural Nepali bridges are dangerous, some more than others! A new bridge required a sacrifice before it was safe to open it — a human sacrifice. When a new bridge was built over a gorge in central Pokhara, one of the young engineers was eventually persuaded that his was the privilege of being that sacrifice. After much delay, he jumped to his death.

Later another bridge was built close to the Shining Hospital. As the foundations were laid, parents kept their children indoors. To avoid the need of human sacrifice a priest stood under that bridge, right arm raised, for three weeks. Ruth went to visit him periodically during that time. Inevitably, his arm became fixed above his head, but the bridge was declared safe.

The land on which the Shining Hospital staff compound was built was just above the place of cremation. It was believed by the Nepalis to be the domain of evil spirits. The land was prayed over by the Christians and claimed for the Lord. These seem strange ideas to us from the West. We equate evil with personal badness but that is but one fruit of the great tree of evil.

Ruth became very aware of the reality of evil. Increasingly she saw people in her outpatient clinic who were troubled by evil spirits. They came for prayer, not medicine, and went away helped. Occasionally a patient would be demon-possessed. People who had been crawling on the floor, acting like animals, were made whole. 'The great need is for discernment, to know when a situation is devil-induced and when it isn't', Ruth commented. The Nepali Christians were often called to pray over these people, casting out the demons in the name of Christ. Missionaries were not immune either. Many were troubled by the powers of evil, causing ill health, irrational fears, depression. Release came when the group met to pray about these matters.

A hostel in the bazaar was rented for the Nepali nurses. According to practice learnt from bitter experience, as the house had previously been dedicated to the Hindu gods, Ruth and several others gathered to pray and sing in each room, casting out any evil influences which might be present, inviting in the living God. As they started to sing, all hell was let loose. A man, armed with a khukri, the Nepali fighting knife, rushed in through the door and started to attack the singers. He seized all the hymn books before being overpowered and thrust down the stairs. They decided to continue singing whilst this man ripped up all the hymn books and Bibles he had taken. As they went from room to room they saw him leave, and then sit on the verandah across the road. Next day he came back, in his right mind, to ask for teaching about the Lord. In the room underneath this disturbance, unknown to anyone, lay a sick woman. During the singing a lightness came over her body and she was healed. Such things happened many times.

The first time Ruth saw another missionary affected was when on holiday with people from a different mission. As Ruth lay in bed, she felt an evil presence. There and then she claimed the protection of the crucified Lord and slept unhindered.

Foolishly I never thought of claiming it for the others. Next morning one of them was foaming at the mouth, refusing to eat, unable to speak. As we prayed, so she became more violent. We didn't know what to do, so we let her be. Next day she seemed calmer, until we approached her. If we tried praying or reading the Bible she threw things at us. She kicked a dog down the stairs.

During the night we heard her packing her bags, and we went out after her. We caught her standing on the edge of a cliff, about to throw herself over. We took her home, sat with her and solidly read the Bible. She settled and we went for a picnic together. When we returned she was worse again, so the reading went on. Eventually she was able to thank God that he had delivered her. After that she was all right.

This was a very persistent attack, however, and on their way back the window of the bus fell in on them, the girl was then bitten by a dog and needed a full course of anti-rabies vaccine, and finally she fell and was concussed. Satan could be seen as a roaring lion seeking someone to devour. The girl had been growing slack in her Christian life, allowing the devil loopholes, of which he made the most. The spiritually careless Christian is in great danger.

Ruth was subject to a particularly horrible onslaught, in her own garden. She woke one morning to find crows flying around. She investigated and discovered, lightly buried, the dismembered leg of a newborn baby. To Nepalis this is a powerful curse directed against the finder, and Ruth was that finder. Next day, the head was found near another house. She knew that such curses certainly worked on the superstitious Nepalis. Having overcome her horror, Ruth called for help and for the police (who never did discover where the body came from), and the group then prayed.

The presence of evil, and the reality of the battle between good and evil, is felt by few in the Christianised countries, though where people turn from the living God to magic and mysticism the problem becomes real once again. Ruth was very concerned at the rising interest in the occult in England, knowing where it would lead.

Surrounded by so much evil it was necessary to have the right protection, and the power and authority to overcome that evil. During the 1960s the charismatic renewal began to make an impact in Pokhara, lifting the group to new levels of praise, worship and prayer. It began when Graham Scott-Brown and his wife Margaret had a new experience of the Holy Spirit whilst on furlough, returning full of enthusiasm.

Some of the younger missionaries were unhappy in the mission, and had started to meet for prayer. As Graham and Margaret shared their experiences with this group, gradually one and another experienced the power of the Holy Spirit in different ways.

The older folk, including Ruth, were apprehensive and

suspicious. Yet gradually they too were changed. Pat O'Hanlon felt the Lord putting his hand on her shoulder and saying, 'It's all right, they are my children,' and had peace about the development.

Ruth went to see Graham about all this. She was very critical. She didn't like it theologically and told Graham so. They talked long into the evening. Ruth left to walk back across the old parade ground to the compound, and as she went she suddenly and totally unexpectedly found herself speaking in tongues. She felt no great emotion about this, but knew the Lord had met her in a new way. The greatest change which ocurred as a result of this renewed experience of God within the group was a willingness to share ups and downs, and the ways in which God was speaking to them or dealing with them. Dullness was replaced with enthusiasm and it was as if everyone was in love with the Lord for the first time.

Newcomers to the group in later years were often deeply touched by the continued vitality and care in the group and were much helped by it. It was for Ruth and many colleagues a renewing experience which changed them. Yet for the group it was the prelude to a time of great trouble.

Ruth never found it easy to relax after long, tiring days. She deliberately did not read letters from home in the evenings, but often read novels. She had the ability to catnap – the secret source of her enormous energy. The space under her string bed was full of medical journals, both read and unopened. Like many colleagues, she struggled to keep up to date.

Ruth loved gardening. On the slope beside the door of her two-roomed thatched house was a beautiful bougainvillea, bought in the Botanical Gardens in Calcutta. Amaryllis grew in the hedgerows. A white jasmine flourished incongruously in an old enamel bucket beside her door, up and over the porch. Pink rain flowers bloomed in the heat and tropical storms. Her strawberries were carefully tended and delicious, enjoying a four-month season. Out of her back window, across the poinsettias red in November, past the bougainvillaea purple in May, was the constantly inspiring view of Fishtail, arguably the world's most beautiful mountain. Inside, African violets abounded, with photos and mementoes of home.

Days off were often spent at the lake, now the haunt of the young world travellers from Australia, Europe and America. Swimming, especially in the hot season, was superb, and paddling across in a dugout canoe, relaxing and good exercise. In the earlier years, out of respect for the scruples of the Nepalis, the missionaries swam dressed in blouses and ankle length sari petticoats. Later, when tourists became more numerous and the Nepalis became used to the sight of scantily-clad white bodies, Ruth and her colleagues too donned swimsuits and delighted in swimming unhindered by folds of wet material.

The constant pressure and unceasing activity took its toll. Ruth Watson spent much of her time ill. She suffered badly from attacks of asthma, and was extremely allergic to cats. Inevitably, cats loved her and sought her out!

Going home on holiday once, she stayed in Kathmandu with a friend who, unfortunately, had a cat. On the flight to Bangkok Ruth began to feel unwell. After a night there, she was worse and was started on treatment immediately prior to the flight to London. During the flight she became so bad that she needed continuous oxygen. At one point during the journey Ruth recalled with great amusement, the oxygen had to be taken away to be bubbled through a tank of fish, which were also suffering.

Asthma apart, Ruth had more than her fair share of illness. Her second furlough in 1964 had not been the success she had planned – lots of exercise, food, blooming health. Instead, she had boil after boil. Her furlough finished, Ruth flew back to Delhi and then on down to the South of India to spend six months learning leprosy surgery. Her health improved, until towards the end of her time there she again had pain and diarrhoea. She ended up in the renowned Christian Medical College in Vellore, under the care of a great expert in tropical sprue, Professor Baker. She settled, and was put on to long-term treatment. Eventually, just before Christmas 1964, Ruth arrived back in Pokhara to a great welcome. It was good to get back – now to get going with all those new skills learnt in India.

Not for long. Within six weeks Ruth entered a crisis not surpassed until her final illness. A tender swelling developed in her neck. She had flown over to Kathmandu expecting a short holiday, but ended up seeing her friend from Patna days, Dr Win Anderson. She whisked Ruth away to see a surgical colleague in the main hospital of the United Mission to Nepal.

They were clearly worried. The lump was removed. The specimen was sent hundreds of miles to Ludhiana in Northern India. A long wait of the sort which stretches faith and patience – then two weeks later, a telegram. It was not malignant, but a rare type of inflammation known as De Quervains Thyroiditis, about which little was then known. Everyone was cheered. It was going to take time but the disease was self-limiting.

Ruth did not improve, however. The other side of her neck became swollen and tender. She was put on to large doses of steroids to dampen the inflammation. She improved intially, but then deteriorated again. There was one compensation in this treatment. It meant that she could for the first time ever stay with her great friend Win Anderson. Win had a cat, but Ruth's terrible allergy to cats was dampened by the steroids, preventing the asthma. Ruth lost weight steadily.

Frustration heightened. Prayer was made, friends laying hands on her in the age-old manner. There was no improvement in her health, but Ruth had peace. She couldn't possibly understand why she was ill, but she could accept it.

Six months after arriving in Shanta Bhawan, Ruth thought she was dying. Her stomach swelled up and she was moved to the British Council in Kathmandu for complete rest and quiet, and put on to TB drugs. She improved, to everyone's delight and surprise, except, strangely, Ruth's. She had got used to the idea of dying, and was looking forward to meeting her Lord. She felt cheated.

It was virtually a year since she had worked. Ruth had learnt much. She saw how deeply people cared. After eight years of hurt there had been time for reconciliation with Hilda, who visited her on the way to nurse her sister in England. Her pride had been tempered, her love of medicine (competing with her love for her Lord) had been surrendered. This pride, and her love of medicine, were her chief stumbling blocks, Ruth felt.

Her health continued to be indifferent. In 1973 after twenty-one years in Nepal, Ruth caught hepatitis, going bright yellow. She again suffered the frustration of being away from the work — this time for two months, and experienced the added indignity of being carried past many staring eyes on a porter's back into the hills for her convalescence. But these periods of forced inactivity were not without profit — a Nepali friend put it in perspective when she said, 'It is wonderful that you have been sick. It's given you time to talk to us!'

# 12
# COLLEAGUES

Illness or no, Ruth was a dynamo. She drove herself, and she drove her colleagues. She gave of the whole of her being, with no reserve. She could not understand those who did less, and, as we have seen, she found it hard to relax. Medicine, caring for the sick and needy who queued up to wait for her, who depended on her, was her great love. She could not understand those who were delighted when the day's work was done, who rejoiced on the wet days in the monsoons when few patients braved the torrential rain. Some of her colleagues needed time to read, to rest, to write – to develop new lines of interest or spend time with their families. While Ruth did such things, too, her priorities were more vigorously defined.

If the work wasn't there, Ruth would unconsciously look for some, and usually found it, to the dismay of her colleagues. Surgery at night found Ruth helping to prepare for it, and cleaning up the theatre after it. She expected others to do the same, and was hurt if they didn't. Delegation was an unknown art to her. To Ruth it meant, 'I'll do it'. She cared nothing for status, delighting to do the menial tasks, even as Jesus washed the disciples' feet. She couldn't understand colleagues who felt that delegation led to efficiency and a more effective ministry.

April, May and June were very hot, very busy months. Dysentery and typhoid were rife. Orthopaedic injuries were abundant as the Nepalis went up trees and down cliffs with their knives, searching the parched land for food for the animals. Outpatients was greatly over-crowded – and every patient had to see the doctor. That was the system. Some mornings one hundred and fifty patients, other days two hundred and fifty patients, queued for hours to see the doctors. It was hot, exhausting work. Then, the staff returned, in the heat of the day, to be found in the operating theatre often after only fifteen minutes for lunch.

Ruth was like a coiled spring. The greater the work-load and the hotter the weather, the faster she went. Extra operations were crammed in. Ruth became more and more deeply immersed, dragging everyone else with her into the maelstrom of activity. Tempers became frayed, tears were shed. Others would almost welcome the news that Ruth had an asthma attack – it gave a needed breathing space. In spite of these frictions her missionary colleagues not only respected her, but had a deep affection for her.

In the midst of all this busyness Ruth still had time for people. She often spent days off with friends, and was available in the evenings for a quiet chat. She loved to cook for herself, inviting friends in occasionally, but when the need came latterly to fulfil the role of 'the senior missonary' and eat in the headquarters, she gladly gave up this pleasure. Indeed, she gladly gave up her lovely room for sick colleagues, who convalesced there. That house, and the one attached next door, were built with money given to Ruth and to Joan Short specifically for the building of a stone house, which otherwise would have been beyond their means.

Meal times in the compound were quaintly formal. They were served by the Nepali kitchen staff who waited at table as the servants would in an English country house. There was a small bell at the top of the table, where Ruth usually sat after Pat O'Hanlon's retirement. A sharp tap on the bell from Ruth would produce a flurry from the kitchen, the clearing of dishes and the arrival of the next course. Meals usually ended up with one or more of Ruth's great store of anecdotes. She was great fun, loving to be in the middle of a crowd, loving a party whenever it came round.

Like many idealistic and deeply committed people Ruth possessed a temper which sometimes got the better of her.

It was felt by the mission leaders that the group should learn more of the Nepali ways and culture. An educated Brahmin man once gave several talks to help them. His chief criticisms were of anger and impatience. Ruth took this very much to heart, knowing it applied to her, and she tried to practise calmness and patience in the crowded, busy outpatients.

Patients often swarmed round the windows, shouting, trying to attract Ruth's attention. On one occasion, in the middle of the series of talks, two or three patients were being examined inside the room. Ruth's patience with those outside was wearing thin and she shooed them frantically away from the windows. One woman was particularly stubborn, and kept coming and shouting.

Eventually, Ruth's patience ran out. She got up, went out, picked the woman up and removed her some distance away.

At the next culture lesson, the Brahmin said how disappointed he was that his lesson had not been learnt. The woman at the window had been his wife!

On other occasions, Ruth threw bowls of water over pestering patients. Nobody minded. The Nepalis recognised that she genuinely loved them, and gave everything for them, and were glad to see her keeping queue-jumpers in order.

Inevitably, some people do not adjust to the particular pressures of missionary life. Ruth, as a senior missionary and doctor, had close dealings with such people. She felt strongly that it was not their fault, and that they were often badly hurt. She laid great responsibility for good selection at the feet of the Home Councils of missions.

In her last months, Ruth agonised over this problem, having seen the problems produced by unsuitable selections.

Unsuitable candidates must be turned down. Of course, this is hard on them, but sending out unsuitable people puts their very real faith under severe attack. They feel, 'God called me, God sent me, God can cope with my problems' and then discover it just isn't like that. Their spirits if not their voices cry out, 'What's happening?', and this is so damaging to their faith.

Mission selection boards need more training in counselling and interview techniques, and ability to probe the unrevealed areas of a person. Certainly people from broken homes are far more liable to have problems than others. But so too are proud people, like myself.

There will never be a perfect system. How then do you help the person who, when out at the battle-front, develops real problems? All around are people also under pressure, coping to a greater or lesser degree.

The mission team needs not only a leader, but also a pastoral figure, a counsellor. This is not easy in a mixed group. The leader may well be a man. What does he know of the problems facing the young or menopausal woman unless he has been trained?

If a woman does have problems, these will certainly be accentuated by the menopause. It often goes unrecognized, and the problem is 'spiritualized'. The missionary feels she is failing the Lord, whereas the real problem is that there aren't enough hormones chasing round the system. Younger colleagues need to be taught about this. Sometimes a year or two at home is needed.

The happy person is, generally, a healthy one. Much of the sickness seen amongst staff in Nepal, expatriate and Nepali, was stress-related. Very often this presented as persistent diarrhoea — such as Ruth herself had experienced in her first term abroad. Again she recognised the need to discern the true nature of the problem. Was it physical or was it spiritual? 'If you love them, you will know,' was advice she found so helpful.

Ruth claimed she didn't get depressed. Certainly at times she felt oppressed with the evil around her. When she did occasionally feel 'down' she chracteristically shrugged it off, got up, rushed around involving herself until the feeling had passed. 'I feel depressed, but please don't show any sympathy,' she would say. Because this was her reaction to feeling 'down', she felt it was possible for others to do the same. If it wasn't hormonal, it was a spiritual matter. Like so many people who have not experienced true depression she had little understanding of the condition which affects every aspect of life and which doesn't respond to shrugging it off, prayer, fasting, or the laying on of hands. There were people she was unable to help. She was a brilliant surgeon, but a poor psychiatrist! Ruth, with her forceful personality and her constant activity, felt that this was the answer for others: 'snapping out of it', saturating life with activity to erase the problems. Those, however, are not solutions available to the truly depressed. Careful counselling and support over a long period are needed.

Her colleagues and friends were a typically mixed group, yet they shared a common love for God and a desire to serve him in Nepal. Some never seemed to have problems, most had times when they needed support and encouragement, a few were ill-suited to the task and unable to cope.

All these were Ruth's responsibility, medically and spiritually – in addition to one million Nepalis. Her slender shoulders were generally broad enough to bear these things, but at times the strain revealed itself in attacks of asthma – as stress-related disease as any.

Each month, the mission set aside a day for prayer, and twice a year General Meetings were held, lasting several days. These were times for fellowship, teaching and prayer, and also times for sharing visions and burdens.

One long-standing colleague, Betty Bailey, had a burning vision, almost a certainty, that leprosy work should begin in the neglected areas of Western Nepal. Another couple had a deep concern for the Tibetan population of the area, and were learning that most difficult language. Ruth wholeheartedly entered into these visions of others.

Among her many friends, Ruth made several deeper, though not exclusive, friendships. One such was with Patricia Hepworth. Trish was secretary to the mission, and she and Ruth encouraged one another in practical ways. When Trish was overwhelmed by accounts Ruth would help her out. They shared a room for several years, and Trish recalled the day when, during a violent rain storm, she found Ruth sitting on her bed having tea with her umbrella up. Both had connections with the Girls' Crusader Union, and with Pat O'Hanlon appeared in the Girl Crusaders' magazine as 'our missionaries'.

In 1965 Trish caught a heavy cold. Surprisingly, she continued to deteriorate. Urgent blood specimens were sent to Kathmandu. Suddenly Ruth realised what had happened. When initially unwell, Trish had been taking simple aspirin-like medicine. Very rarely the drug caused the bone marrow to dry up breaking the body's natural defence mechanism.

Ruth knew there was little hope, and nothing she could do for her friend. The nurses took turns to sit with Trish, who was delirious. One morning, shortly after eating a light breakfast and seeming slightly better, Trish suddenly collapsed. Ruth and Joan were called and sat with her as she died.

For the Nepali Christians, for the missionaries, and especially for Ruth there was great sadness and a deep sense of loss, accompanied by equally great joy that Trish had gone to meet her Lord. In silence Ruth returned to finish her clinic. The funeral took place that evening at Green Pastures as the sun was setting.

Ruth loved her work, the hospital and medicine; but her deepest love was for people. Her great concern was to reach them.

Tibetan refugees, chased from their homeland by the invading Chinese, added colour to the Shining Hospital. In 1951 the Chinese moved into Tibet, a country always under Chinese suzerainty, yet in all other ways totally separate in culture and religion.

Tibet, 'the roof of the world', that windswept tableland in central Asia, 16,000 feet above sea level, is the source of some of the world's greatest rivers, the Indus, Ganges, Brahmaputra, Mekon and Yangtze. Ethnically the people are related to the Mongols, and are totally different from the Chinese, though the languages have common roots.

Tibetan religion is an animistic form of Buddhism organised by the lamas, or priests, with the Dalai Lama as their spiritual head. Prior to the Chinese take-over he was also the ruler, and all men, beasts and land belonged to him. The people are mainly herdsmen, rearing oxen, yaks, sheep and horses. Wool is spun, dyed and woven. Some cultivate the land. All are great tea-drinkers and their favourite dish, *tsampa*, is a paste made from roast barley and tea.

During the 1950s China increased pressure on Tibet to

conform to her principles, and eventually in 1959 there was a general uprising[1]. Ruthlessly crushed by the Chinese, the Dalai Lama fled to India. From there he continues to govern his people in exile, despite India's reluctance to recognise him. The Tibetans have maintained their separateness, refusing to intermarry, taking orders only from the Dalai Lama, hoping one day to return to Tibet and establish the Buddhist way there.

That dreadful winter of 1959 saw thousands of Tibetans fleeing through the high Himalayan passes into northern India and Nepal. Many died on the way, many more on arrival, from cold, malnutrition and disease. Pokhara, connected with Tibet by the main trade route to the north through the Kali Gandaki gorge, became one centre for these refugees, Kathmandu being the other. Two camps were established with international aid. The Swiss, in particular, felt a great affinity with the Tibetans and established self-help centres, to make carpets, coats and other cottage industries. Later, as refugees continued to trickle down in the 1970s, two further camps were set up.

Tibetans were always first in the queue at the Shining Hospital, waiting for numbers to be issued. Some would stay overnight in the busy season to be sure of being seen. It was necessary for the Shining Hospital to put a ceiling on the numbers to be seen in out-patients each day, though emergencies were always seen. Some two thousand Tibetans lived around Pokhara and many of them were very sick. For the first three or four years after arrival in Pokhara, they had little resistance to local disease, and became seriously ill with dysentery and tuberculosis. Nutrition was poor and accommodation overcrowded, ensuring a very stormy time. There is no doubt that the hospital made a major contribution to their overall well being.

Although tuberculosis was rife amongst them, leprosy was rare. Unlike the Nepalis who were very fertile, the

Tibetans were subfertile, having small families and rarely needing family planning. They were model patients, always doing as they were told. The practical problem for Ruth, with the women, was their clothes. Summer or winter, they always wore layers of heavy wool garments. To examine a chest or abdomen was a long, slow task. And as the layers were peeled off down to the rarely-changed inner garments, the windows needed to be wide open! But despite these minor problems Ruth loved these folk.

Attractive and affectionate as they are, they can also be cruel. Several Tibetans have shown interest in Christianity and a few have become Christians. But the opposition to them is enormous. At least one is known to have been poisoned and probably others also, for this is the way the Tibetans deal with their traitors. God's church, strong and expanding amongst the Nepalis, made small progress amongst these refugee people until October 1981, when the first ever Tibetan Christian Conference was held in Kathmandu and several were baptised.

The other group of despised, rejected people much loved by Ruth were the leprosy sufferers.

Nepalis believe that leprosy is a curse from the gods. It was usual for sufferers to be thrown out of their villages and stripped of their land and possessions. Of all diseases, this was most greatly to be feared. Inevitably, sufferers sought to keep the tell-tale signs hidden for as long as possible. Many ended up hopeless in government asylums where the law of the jungle was the rule.

Leprosy is caused by bacteria closely related to the tuberculosis bacteria, but is much less infectious. In those people with no resistance to the disease, the bacteria spread in fantastic numbers in the skin, affecting the nose and eyebrows, and gradually destroying the nerves of sensation. The end result is the tragically deformed patient with no fingers or toes, no nose, thick cheeks and no eyebrows. Those with greater resistance may suffer damage to only one nerve, normally the ulnar nerve in the region of the elbow where it can be felt thick and hard. This causes the typical claw hand of leprosy.

Many of these patients can be helped. All can be cured of the disease by modern medicine and today, after years of hard effort, former leprosy sufferers are allowed back to their villages, once the disease has been eradicated. Surgery had much to offer.

In 1956 Green Pastures Leprosy Hospital was established, on the site of a former leprosarium. Early patients were badly crippled, needing shelter as much as anything. The psychological damage, often as bad as the physical, meant that people, though cured, often could not be persuaded to leave the shelter of the hospital.

In the early 1970s Ruth, Betty Bailey and others walked extensively in the far west region of Nepal, looking for a chain of headquarters from which to run a leprosy control programme. In the early days, many patients, hearing of a place of hope, walked for several weeks on their deformed feet from those isolated valleys deep in the midst of remote stretches of steep hills. Application was made to the government to start leprosy and possibly TB work in that neglected area. For years nothing was heard. Then suddenly government permission was granted and the mission's programme was integrated into a government/World Health Organisation programme. Control for half of the country was passed to the mission as a long-term ongoing programme. Faith becomes reality.

Ruth had little experience of leprosy surgery and following her furlough in 1964 she went straight to Karigiri in South India to the hospital established by the world's leading leprosy surgeon, Paul Brand. Dr Brand, son of a British missionary, was born in India and trained as a builder and carpenter before studying medicine. He used his carpentry skills to develop operations to help the leprosy sufferer, changing good tendons for those of paralysed muscles and then teaching the patient to re-use them. He used this technique on hands, and on 'drop foot'. By transplanting skin he built new eyebrows and recreated the power to close the eyes and blink. Using bone from the hip he rebuilt noses.

In her six months in Karigiri Ruth Watson learned these skills. She returned to Pokhara, her new knowledge now available to leprosy sufferers who came to her for help. It was no instant success story. Some operations failed. But many patients were helped. She had also learnt the vital importance of hand exercises, and of good shoes to protect the insensitive feet. Later years saw the Green Pastures farm develop to provide food and work for the patients. Later still a larger rehabilitation unit was built to teach patients how to earn their living, despite severe deformities.

Ruth visited Green Pastures most weeks. In the early days she used to walk or cycle the six-mile journey. On one occasion when she was ill she was determined to go. She instructed a porter to cut away the back of his *doko*[2] and make a seat in it. Placing her cushion in it she instructed him to carry her on his back to Green Pastures, her black umbrella providing the shade. After three days there he carried her back. Later Ruth learned to drive – in a hectic few weeks in London, to everyone's amazement and not a little disbelief. When the road was built she then drove down in the Mobile Clinic, a diesel Land Rover, which had an enormous spare tyre on the top of the bonnet. The journey had its hazards, and passengers sometimes wished they had walked. The track crossed the airstrip, then over a short, very narrow bridge above a 200foot gorge. It was just wide enough for the Land Rover, with Ruth straining up to see over the spare tyre and her passengers quaking in their seats. After that it was extremely bumpy, but safe.

In 1973 a German surgeon, Paul Kalthoff, arrived to take care of the rapidly developing leprosy programme. Ruth, saturated with work in the Shining Hospital, was delighted to hand over to him.

The 1970s saw a great 'wind of change' sweeping the developing world. Nepal was not excluded. Plans were well advanced to build a new 'proper' Shining Hospital with aid money from Germany. Building was about to start. The original hospital had totally outgrown its forty beds – often sixty patients would be staying. The working conditions were poor. The out-patient department, with only two consulting rooms for seeing fifty thousand patients per year, was totally inadequate, as were the operating theatre and maternity hut.

Suddenly, permission from the government was withdrawn. Rumours were rife that all mission hospitals were to be taken over by the government or closed. One group of non-medical language specialists were given two weeks to leave the country. Nepali Christians were watched and some arrested. In Pokhara several were imprisoned for some months. One pastor was in jail for more than a year. It looked as if the days of the Shining Hospital were numbered.

Then came the request, 'Please don't build a new Shining Hospital. Put the money into the new government hospital in Pokhara.' There was much debate about this, but little alternative. Fortunately, the German donors agreed, with some conditions. The building and the running were to be done jointly by mission and government.

For Ruth this represented a major change. From being in a totally independent organisation, and very much boss, she was now required to negotiate with and work alongside the government. She accepted the new situation with few reserves. It presented new possibilities – a whole new world of people to share her Lord with. She was on excellent terms with her medical colleagues throughout Nepal, often attending the annual Nepal Medical Conference, and speaking at it on several occasions.

New opportunities and possibilities, and more work. Hospital plans to approve; the layout of out-patients, wards and particularly the theatre on which to advise. Equipment lists to be submitted. Construction board meetings to be held. And against that background, the wonder of what the future held for the Shining Hospital and its officially untrained staff. That was her greatest concern – for the Nepali people whose livelihood was threatened.

So came the wind of change. Sometimes such winds die down. Not this time. A totally unexpected change lay close at hand.

## Notes

[1] For fascinating accounts of Tibet in the 1950s, see *Seven Years in Tibet* by Heinrich Harrer, and *When Iron Gates Yield* by Geoffrey Bull.
[2] A cone-shaped basket woven from bamboo and carried by a strap from the forehead.

# 13
# CHANGE

February in Nepal is the most glorious of months. Day after day is clear and bright. The Himalayas, clothed in perpetual snow, gleam brightly down, reflecting the light of the sun with pinks in the mornings, and red and purple at sunset. Nights are still cold, even down to freezing in exposed fields, and day-time temperatures are up to 80°F. It is a beautiful month for tourism, especially for trekking, and Phewa Tal, the lake in the Pokhara Valley, fills up with young people from across the Western world, savouring Asia, swimming and boating and often trading in hash.

For the people of Nepal, February is an easier month. The rice harvest has long been gathered in, and the threshed rice safely stored in sacks. In the valleys such as Pokhara, and on the terraced hillsides, it is still another month before the ploughing and sowing begins again for the maize crop. Mustard seed has been sown, and fields burst bright yellow with these brilliant flowers, growing on seemingly parched dry soil, then falling, leaving the seed to ripen.

It is a month when men sit around talking, putting the world to rights, or buy and sell houses or cattle. Women-folk can be spared temporarily, and many find their way down to the hospital that shines. They often bring their children, some of whom have been burnt during the cold winter nights.

The usual diseases, dysentery, typhoid, even TB seem less common, and the medical wards are fairly empty. For the surgeon, however, these are the peak months, when people have time for non-urgent surgery. Ruth once took her holiday in January, but was told by her patients, in no uncertain terms, not to do so again!

The most difficult cases in surgery were always skin grafts on children. Time was crucial. A small baby under anaesthetic, totally undressed, quickly became cold. Taking split skin grafts from the tiny thighs to put on to other areas newly cleared of scar tissue required great skill and speed. Extensive bleeding from these large raw areas occurred in the little children. Skilled team work was necessary to minimise the risk from anaesthetic, cold, and blood loss which too easily could prove fatal.

Ruth Watson can have had few equals in this field, and the results were remarkable – at least as good as in the best of plastic surgical units in the West. The sunshine must have had a major part to play in these outstanding successes.

It was during one of these afternoon operating sessions that Dr Marilyn Whillas arrived from Australia. Late in 1975 she had offered herself to the Australian Home Council of the International Nepal Fellowship, as the NEB had now been named, for short term service. Already qualified in medicine, she had trained at the Melbourne Bible Institute, and was just finishing her present medical post. With Dr Val Inchley on furlough in Britain and Dr Mary Thomson working away in a village on a TB and leprosy programme, Ruth Watson was coping with the women's side alone, and finding the pressure of work, especially the out-of-hours maternity work, increasingly hard to cope with. Shortly after putting her bags in her room, Marilyn was taken up to meet the Kanchi Doctor. Ruth, typically, had just finished an operation and emerged from the operating hut into the bright sunshine outside, her apron still red with the fresh blood stains of the operation, to give her new colleague an enormous smile, an outstretched arm, and a big greeting.

This particular February, however, was not one of the happiest. Tensions had arisen in the hospital and in the misson. For the first time the government hospital had a trained surgeon and anaesthetist, and they were able to cope with much more than before. Prior to this, the Shining Hospital had been forced to concentrate on traditional approaches to medicine – through surgery and wards and outpatient clinics. It was not possible to go out into the community to try to prevent diseases occurring – the pressure of those already sick absorbed all the time the staff had.

The question was again being asked, 'Who is my patient?' Was it the man who sat in front of me with dysentery asking for help, or was it that milling mass of people in the bazaar outside, drinking contaminated water, eating an inadequate diet, lacking basic sanitation? Mission hospitals had traditionally concentrated on healing the sick, but newer members were feeling that preventing the disease was equally important. Debate and argument raged. Some newcomers were not tactful. The establishment seemed entrenched, and threatened by the implications of a change.

Ruth and one of her younger medical colleagues had an ongoing sharp disagreement – partly over these suggested changes, partly due to the unwillingness of the younger to be constantly on call when his family needed him. Conversation between the two was kept to a necessary minimum – there seemed little to talk about except for those things which divided. Ruth had moved camps. From being the young doctor desperately trying to establish herself and provide the

109

service she was so capable of giving against the background of a domineering but outdated colleague, she found herself appearing to strive to maintain the *status quo*.

But Ruth was *for* change. The question was, 'How quickly and how much?' While debte raged, nothing changed in the mission. Outside in the wider world, during the early seventies, mission philosophy was changing. The big medical institutions were giving way to the preventive work of vaccination programmes, to 'under fives' clinics, and to improving water and sanitation. National and international politics were changing too, and throughout the world nationalism was marching forward, tending to throw out the good of colonial influences with the bad.

Nepal was no exception. The International Nepal Fellowship, with other missions, came within an ace of being asked to leave. Some mission groups *were* suddenly removed from Nepal.

For Ruth, these problems created new tensions. She loved surgery, and was outstanding in her practice of it. The people loved her, and despite the presence of an excellent surgeon in the government hospital they still, in the main, came to her for their surgery. They would have been unable to understand why she should stop. Yet surgery was labour-intensive. One operation tied up two doctors and three nursing staff. Had extra staff, national and mission, been forthcoming, a preventive medical programme could have begun alongside, using the goodwill built up over the years. Indeed, one clinic had long been established in the town with this as its main aim. But as urban drift caused Pokhara's population to double, then treble in ten years, this clinic was reaching only a few.

Such were the dilemmas and tensions facing Ruth, as senior missionary, when Marilyn Whillas arrived. Who could have guessed that, over the next four years, Marilyn was to guide the Shining Hospital through its traumas, superbly supported by senior members of the hospital? Megs Owen, Jean Morgan and Kerrie Worboys all worked and trained by day, and prepared and planned by night, so that by 1980 the Shining Hospital had undergone radical transformation, and had taken those leaps forward so long debated in previous years.

Ruth quickly set about training Lyn Whillas in the Pokhara ways of doing things.

It is a vast jump, especially for the young doctor, from the world of readily-available sophisticated equipment and investigations where money is no object, into the harsh world of limited resources in time, money, equipment and manpower. Some barely make it.

Lyn loved learning with Ruth, and quickly learned basic surgical skills. She caught something of Ruth's love and care for people. Even in a busy clinic Ruth would find time to stop and pray with someone she felt had basically a spiritual rather than a physical need. This made a deep impact on her young colleague.

Lyn had been in Pokhara about three weeks when Ruth suddenly started to get headaches. At first she told no one, doing as she had always done, trying to fight it off. She was busy. There was underlying tension. Teaching Lyn was an added chore which slowed her down. One morning one of the sisters went into Ruth's consulting room to ask about a patient. Ruth was sitting, cradling her head in her hands.

'I feel terrible. I must just sit quiet a minute; it will soon pass off,' she said.

The first any of her medical colleagues heard of this was almost two weeks after the headaches started. It was a casual aside during an operating session and her colleagues thought little of it. Wasn't she under pressure? Wasn't she overworking? Wasn't she as usual taking on herself what ought to be delegated? When had she last had a holiday? That was due now. Small wonder she was having headaches. A colleague checked her blood pressure, performed a quick basic examination and concluded this was migraine. Ruth was given tablets for that.

One of the twice-yearly General Meetings of the mission was again upon them, bringing the pleasure of reunion with friends from other more isolated bases, but also extra work as meetings for business and prayer were fitted into the full schedule of the hospital. Fairly typically, Ruth found lots of work to do during that week. She had been persuaded that she should bring forward her holiday, and was preparing for that. A friend from school days had arrived, providing the companion she needed for a trekking holiday.

'You must get your headaches looked into in Kathmandu, Ruth' she was told.

'What I need is a good holiday. If I have still got them when I get back, I'll go then,' she promised.

On the Sunday after the General Meeting had finished, a small group was being driven to the airstrip to return to the leprosy outstation in Ghorahi. Discussion was about the 'Shining' and its need for change.

'I can't see any way it can really change as long as Ruth is there,' said one of the older missionaries. 'It isn't so much that Ruth won't change, but that the people won't let her.'

Unwittingly, Ruth was becoming a hindrance to the inevitable changes which development brings with it.

As this discussion was going on, Ruth, just six miles away, despite being unwell, insisted on doing her Sunday duty in the Shining Hospital. As she had done for nearly twenty-five years, Ruth crossed the cattle grid into the hospital – going to those in need on her day off to help them where she could.

She saw the emergencies in out-patients, and went round the wards checking that all was well, adjusting this treatment, changing that, encouraging the depressed woman in the corner of the ward. She left to return to her room for coffee – and could not find her way out of the hospital. One half of her visual field had completely gone. She called to one of the sisters. Alarmed, the sister took Ruth by the arm and led her out of the hospital, over the cattle grid, past the pipal tree and into the compound gates.

Lyn Whillas was called to see Ruth, she examined her carefully and thoroughly, discussing with Ruth what she found.

'You have completely lost your vision on the left hand side.' She told Ruth what she already knew. 'The discs in your eyes are a bit blurred. You must go to Kathmandu and be seen. No holiday now.'

Ruth looked up at her with tears in her eyes.

'Do you think it could be a brain tumour?' she asked gently.

The silence was short as Lyn assessed her answer.

'It could be,' she said. 'You must get it looked into.'

Ruth wept quietly. Tears of distress for what lay ahead, tears for all that she would leave behind. Tears as she remembered her beloved Nepalis and colleagues.

She knew in her heart from that moment she would never return. She knew she had finished her course in Nepal. There were times later when she thought of returning, but they never persisted. She knew God was moving her on.

Lyn and Ruth kept these things to themselves. Arrangements were made for Ruth to fly next day to Kathmandu, with her close friend Pat Frazer, only recently returned from furlough, as companion. Few in Pokhara knew what Lyn knew. The girl had great courage as she faced this honestly with her senior missionary. Ruth's whole illness in Nepal covered only three weeks.

For a short time Ruth cried. Then she worked through that day in her room, tidying up, returning things borrowed, writing the odd letter — attempting to put her affairs in order. In retrospect they were poignant moments for those who shared that last day in Pokhara with her. On that day Joyce Deaville, in charge of the mission compound for several years, told Ruth of her engagement to Richard O'Dell. Ruth was the first to know.

A small party saw Ruth off to the airport on Monday. No singing crowd, no final emotive prayers, no handshaking and waving, no garland of flowers for Ruth. Just a rattly old Land Rover. No one realised. Everyone expected Ruth back in a couple of weeks after a much-needed holiday. Ruth knew otherwise. The one who, probably more than any other, had given all of herself for the people of Nepal, dying to her own ambitions that they might live, went away unnoticed.

In Kathmandu, Pat took Ruth straight up to the United Mission Hospital at Shanta Bhawan. She was much worse and could not walk unassisted.

She was fully examined. A look inside the eye at the place where the optic nerve enters was the crucial test. It was very swollen — a sign of greatly increased pressure in the brain. John Dickinson, physician at Shant Bhawan, was in no doubt. 'I think you have some sort of tumour in your head. That's the cause of your headaches and loss of balance. You must go at once to England. There's nothing to be done here.' Ruth was in fact in great pain, and in real danger from dying from this pressure. John gave some treatment to reduce the pressure.

Frantic arrangements were made for the flight home. Next day, Ruth, with Pat as her companion, took the next step — out of Nepal, into a world of suffering. Yet out of it was to come great joy and rejoicing.

# 14
# FINALE

The day after arriving at Heathrow, Ruth was in the Hospital for Nervous Diseases in Queen's Square, London. She was a little better; the treatment given her in Kathmandu had reduced the pressure on her brain.

A week later, just ten days after leaving Pokhara and yet a world away, Ruth went into the operating theatre and had a huge malignant tumour removed from the right side of her brain. Such surgery produces real dilemmas for the surgeon. He longs to remove as much malignant tissue as he can, and yet preserve as much normal brain tissue as he is able. Ruth's tumour had already spread beyond operable realms, but the surgeon attempted to remove as much as he could, to be followed by radiotherapy.

Ruth made an uneventful recovery from the surgery, but found she had distressing and incapacitating handicaps. She could walk and talk with no problem. At first sight, her visitors were relieved to find her so intact. If anything she appeared to be too cheerful. She wanted to sing, and as the ward was nearly empty, she did. A hymn in Nepali came out perfectly. She still had problems seeing things on the left side, but that improved and could be coped with. What was not immediately obvious to her visitors was that more subtle areas had been damaged.

Ruth had lost her visual memory. She could not recognise people. Everyone appeared the same ugly blob. Shown pictures of friends, or of her beautiful Nepali mountains, she had no idea of who or what they were. Frequently, and at times embarrassingly, she mistook people for others – not least when she thought the doctor was the chaplain and entered into a delightful conversation about the goodness of God with no knowledge that the one listening was a stranger to such matters.

This problem slowly improved over the next few months. But though her memory for past events was sharp, present events were quickly forgotten. It made meaningful conversation a problem as she often repeated what had just been said. Writing was a greater effort. In a letter to the mission she explained this:

> Talking is much easier than writing. The trouble with writing is that I cannot read it back with understanding. I know this sounds stupid but it is due to loss of visual recall. As I read or write each word the one before disappears from my mind so that though I can technically read, I cannot remember what I have read, even for one paragraph.

A further severe handicap, not immediately obvious, was that she could not remember her way around a ward or a house. She would try to find her way to the bathroom and fail. Having been taken there, she could not find her way back. This meant she could not go anywhere on her own without being totally lost.

She also lost all sense of time. This was a peculiar experience – one unknown and unimaginable to those of us so bound to mealtimes, bedtimes, getting-up times, and the constant intrusion of the clock into our lives. Ruth lived some seven months after her surgery, yet how long was that to her? Time had gone. In one very real sense, she was experiencing eternity whilst still living on earth.

All these new experiences required adjustments; less than a month before she had been busy operating in the beautiful Himalayas. Amazingly, Ruth took these handicaps, worked at them, adjusted to them and triumphed over them. Indeed, of all the struggles and triumphs of her life, this was the greatest.

Whilst Ruth was still in Queen's Square Hospital, the doctors told her that she would never be able to operate again. It was a devastating experience for one whose first love was surgery. Everything seemed to be taken away. Everything except her faith in God which had stood the test of the years and was now being tested more severely than ever before. Her faith stood firm – for her God was firm.

Very shortly after that news came a letter, a copy of one which had arrived in Nepal just after she had left. Ruth had been elected a Fellow of the Royal College of Surgeons. New Fellows are elected by the college each year. Most budding surgeons have to sweat away at their exams whilst doing their regular work. The pass rate is low, the standard required is high. Occasionally an eminent person is made an Honorary Member. But each year about six people are elected as Fellows, without examination. These are often people whose lives have been dedicated to surgery, often in overseas countries. It is a great honour, a mark of true worth.

The award crowned her dedicated service to the people of Nepal. It was an accolade from her contemporaries in comfortable England. Of course it was a wonderful encouragement in depressing circumstances. It was a fit award with perfect timing.

In July 1976, wearing a wig, and with her proud elderly mother to support her, Ruth went, robed, for the presentation of her FRCS. Few present knew that her work had been prematurely ended.

Following her surgery Ruth was transferred nearer to her home in the Cotswolds, to Oxford for radiotherapy. This made it much easier to see her mother, and put her into close touch again with her old university friend, Dr Ken Tomlinson and his wife Hazel. Ken had spent two periods in Nepal, the first with Ruth at the Shining Hospital in 1969. What they had seen there of the love of Christ so actively demonstrated had proved to be a life-changing experience for the whole Tomlinson family. Now Ken and Hazel were to prove a consistent help to Ruth. She frequently stayed with them and went out visiting with them. Their kindness was a vital factor in the triumph of Ruth's final days.

Sir Michael Sobell House was situated in a quiet corner of the Churchill Hospital, Oxford, looking out over a neighbouring golf course. It was designed particularly to help those with chronic pain and disability, usually with terminal malignant disease.

Ruth Watson was an early patient. She spent two periods in her last six months in the unit and found much help and care there. This was the base to which she returned after weekends away with family or friends. It was whilst a patient here that Ruth went through the blackest period of her life, following her radiotherapy.

In common with other patients, Ruth was put on to anti-epileptic drugs following her major brain surgery, to prevent fits. As she had done previously with other drugs, Ruth reacted excessively, unknowingly.

She began to have severe hallucinations. She was disoriented in time and space.

For long hours she thought about the reality of God. She thought through all angles, and to her great distress proved to her logical mind that God did not exist. She was engulfed in overwhelming panic.

'Get the doctor. I must have the doctor. Get him quick!'

The doctor, himself a Christian who knew the reality of God, stood at her bedside.

'Christ is risen, Christ is risen, Christ is risen . . .' he quietly repeated time and again until the truth and reality of that broke through to Ruth and she settled and believed it.

This was *the* crisis. Soon after this the drug was stopped and her last months were spent joyfully. Never again was there doubt about the reality of her Lord.

Others saw this triumph. Nurses sent a difficult patient to see her, and afterwards reported that he had changed. Friends, rather fearful to visit one so handicapped, feeling inadequate to express themselves, found themselves being encouraged, often challenged, by her brightness. She began again to attempt to pick up the threads of life, to write letters, plan ahead, even to think of a return to Nepal. Particularly, she determined to set out her experiences for others to learn from. Many hours were spent with the tape recorder, reviewing her life and experiences. She looked long and hard at missionary situations, examining reasons for failures, areas of weakness. She retained to the end a zealous spirit, and eager body, and a well-stocked mind. She longed to help those who would come after.

Ruth's sister Jill was a great help and comfort. Though living fifty miles away, in Tower Hamlets, where she was headmistress in a Junior School, Jill spent most weekends with Ruth and their mother, who was still living on her own in the tiny Cotswold village. A friend made transcripts from Ruth's tapes for future use, and passed them on to Jill.

Only a year previously, the strain of nursing her failing father many miles from her place of work had ended for Jill. Now her sister needed her care. Ruth had been with her father when he died – a long, slow illness from a gradually failing heart, which often left him very breathless. His suffering had deeply distressed Ruth and later, when she knew her own death was near, she had a great panic one night in the unit. She had no fear of death, but she did fear dying. Especially dying as her father had, of breathlessness. One night she awoke with asthma — which bothered her to the end — and in a great panic.

'I'm dying. You must get my sister.'

Despite reassurances the panic continued and Jill had to be called from the other side of London in the middle of the night.

After some months of apparent progress, there was evidence that the tumour had regrown. Ruth was told of this and accepted it. Arrangements had been made for the recording of a BBC programme, looking at how a doctor faces her own death. Ruth was glad to continue her ministry of encouragement.

She had one last desire. Though she had been baptised as a child, and later confirmed into the Church of England, Ruth had always had a desire to be baptised as a believer. This was no impulse, and now, in the warmth of the church she had regularly attended during her illness in Oxford, Ruth asked for baptism. At the service she spoke of her experience of God, of his call to her, and lessons she had learnt. She had also had a visit from Hilda Steele, reinforcing the reconciliation of years previously.

One of the last letters she wrote shows a deterioration of her thought pattern but a continuing commitment to medicine, the Third World, and above all to her God. It was to Dr Denis Burkitt, a leading researcher into causes of cancer.

Do encourage all young doctors going abroad to look for opportunities for research in developing countries. The material is immense . . . I was sorry not to be able to give you more help in your research projects whilst in Nepal. In some ways I would like to begin life all over again, as I realise how much more could have been done. But it looks as though I shall soon be 'over the river' as I have a recurrence of a brain tumour. I look forward to a joyful reunion with you as well as seeing the Lord as he really is.

There were thirteen days left for Ruth when she wrote that. She had started to deteriorate.

The medical director of the unit sat down with Ruth one day. Between them, they agreed that she should stop the steroid treatment which had been started in Kathmandu, and allow nature to take its course.

On November 9th her pioneer colleague, Joan, now married and living nearby, visited her and wrote 'Ruth was still very peaceful, but much quieter, almost drowsy.'

She went into a coma.

Back in Pokhara, one of the Nepali nurses came to work confused. 'I had a dream last night, and I saw God taking Kanchi Doctor to be with him.'

And so it was. On November 15th 1976 Ruth Watson, better known to those who had received most from her as Kanchi Doctor, died. She was just fifty.

# POSTSCRIPT

Ruth wrote her final letter to her Nepali friends and missionary colleagues on October 20th.

*I expect you know by now that the tumour in my brain has grown again, and that I am not given long to live, but I want to write and tell you that the love of God is just as real to me as ever it has been, and it is this love of God that I long to share with you in Pokhara. You know that is why I really came to Pokhara, not just to minister to sick bodies, but to help you to understand that God loves you — loves you so much that he gave his Son, the Lord Jesus Christ to die for you. And as I wait these last few weeks here on earth, my one prayer is that in Nepal many, many, will come to know this wonderful truth.*

*I have a lovely painting of a Nepali in my room which reminds me all day to think of you and pray for you. I have letters with news but would love to hear more from you.*

*I am hoping that one day there will be in book form some of the experiences of the last twenty-five years in Nepal. All that I have learned from you, dear friends, in seeing you actually develop and your medical work increase. My greatest desire is that your medical work should not just be scientific medical work, but filled with God's love for people, and that the only way we know he loves us is that he let Jesus Christ, his Son, die for us.*

*With very much love to all my friends in Pokhara.*

# EPILOGUE

In the years following Ruth's death, many of the visions she had, for the church and the medical work in Nepal were being fulfilled.

The Shining Hospital steadily made the transformation from the major hospital to a health post and TB centre by 1984, transferring all its doctors to the newly built Gandaki Zonal Hospital, built almost exactly on the site of those huts where the first ever operations and clinics were carried out in 1952. Ruth's colleague in the 1970s, Val Inchley, has continued with Ruth's vigour and vision in seeking as excellent a centre as money and staffing would allow in the new two hundred bed hospital jointly run by Government and mission.

Leprosy sufferers throughout the Western half of Nepal are increasingly finding help. The Control programme, in its infancy in 1976, has grown enormously, with many young Nepalis being trained in the diagnosis and treatment of this most feared disease. Today they trudge in teams from village to village, health post to health post, as new Districts slowly open in the Far West Region. Referral centres staffed by mission personnel and highly trained Nepalis care for the more complicated cases. Green Pastures continues as a centre for deformed leprosy sufferers.

What would have gladdened Ruth's heart most would be the growth of the church. From the beginning the church has been led by Nepalis, who have made their own decisions on the way the church should be ordered. The role of the mission staff has been to stand alongside, to encourage and support – a role in which Ruth was masterful. In recent years the church has continued to know persecution, and always there have been some believers, from different areas, imprisoned for their faith. This is one reason why the sects have had such little impact in Nepal.

Yet the church grows excitingly. It is a church which loves its king and country, whose members seek to be amongst the best of citizens, yet time and again come up against a culture so steeped in Hinduism that a stand for Christ is needed. In 1984, there are some 150 recognised groups meeting with 15,000 members, and also many small, lonely, isolated groups of two or three. The church, as all churches, has its problems and its disagreements, yet in thirty years it has spread hope and love and life throughout this needy land.

'As I wait these last few weeks on earth, my one prayer is that many, many will come to know this wonderful truth.' That prayer is being increasingly answered.

# THE INTERNATIONAL NEPAL FELLOWSHIP TODAY

*The Shining Hospital, together with all that it stood for, and all those who worked in it, became like a seed; although sown to die, from it sprang much fruit. In the early years Green Pastures Leprosy Hospital grew out of the Shining Hospital Clinic and developed a leprosy control programme which has lasted for fifteen years, and still continues, covering half the country of Nepal and touching eight million people. The Community Health Programme sprang from the clinics run by Shining Hospital and their development into bazaar based clinics. The TB Control Project started as one of the many clinics of the Shining Hospital and is now a separate entity, part of the overall plan to control one of the country's major diseases. After ten long years, the merger with the Government Hospital in Pokhara is at last beginning to take place. The out-patients and casualty departments opened in March 1984 not with speeches, cutting of tape and other panoply, but with the doors opening and the patients starting to pour in. The Shining Hospital has started a new phase in its life.*

*It is illegal to preach the gospel in Nepal, but the lives of men and women committed to Christ can speak louder than any words. People such as Ruth Watson make a lasting impression. One life given to the*

Lord, today as then, can have real significance in helping those in desperate need and bringing life and hope to many.

Nepal is one of the most rapidly changing countries in the world, leaping from a medieval serfdom before 1950 into the twentieth century. Ideas and ways of working are constantly changing and the INF as a Mission needs to be speaking to those changing ideas and involved in them. It is not easy on any count to live in one of the poorest countries in the Third World, to be surrounded by desperate need and to be involved in constant change. Yet here there is opportunity today to be involved in the Lord's work, in prayer, in giving and in going.

Even though the Shining Hospital does not function in the way it did in Ruth's day, its work goes on. The spirit of compassion continues in serving leprosy patients, in reaching and teaching the man and woman in the street through community health, the TB programme and in the running of the Gandaki Zonal Hospital. In fact, there is greater opportunity today than ever before. Recent negotiations with the government have opened up many new possibilities and the INF is looking to the Lord to double the size of the Mission in the coming seven years and for new opportunities to open up in the Mid West and Far West of Nepal. Doctors and nurses are needed, as are administrators, accountants, secretaries and people with many practical skills. So too are those who will faithfully pray and provide the financial resources. The work of the Lord continues in Nepal and help is needed today.

Peter Hitchin
June 1984